THE NOMADIC BOYS

The Gay Guide to Travelling with Pride

OUT *in the* WORLD

Stefan Arestis & Sebastien Chaneac

PAVILION

EUROPE 18

ASIA 64

SOUTH AMERICA 120

NORTH AMERICA *142*

THE MIDDLE EAST + AFRICA *160*

OCEANIA *176*

INTRODUCTION

"Are you guys mad?!"... This was the common reaction from our family and friends in 2014, when we announced that we were going to leave our lives and jobs in London for a big trip in Asia – for an indefinite period of time, with no plan to return.

*T*ravel has been at the heart of our relationship since we first met in 2009. For years, we talked about leaving it all behind and seeing the world together. We spent several years saving and planning and by 2014 we felt confident enough to make the big leap and go for it. We knew the journey ahead wouldn't be easy, especially as a gay couple travelling around the world, and our loved ones worried for us too.

> *"But what will you eat? Where will you sleep? What if you get mugged? What if they beat you up for being gay?!"*

As a way to reassure our family and friends, we set up our blog, Nomadic Boys, so they could follow along on our journey, laugh at our photos, and know that we were doing okay. Nomadic Boys has become our greatest achievement so far. It is our baby. Our pride and joy. But most importantly, it has elevated our relationship and given us both a newfound purpose.

Nomadic Boys has become one of the prime online resources for gay travel. We publish our content to inspire and help fellow gay travellers plan fun and safe trips for themselves, and by sharing our own experiences (both good and bad!) you know what to expect before going away – and we are loving every second!

This book is our love letter to gay travel – our LGBTQ+ bucket list. We've written it from our first-person perspective, taking it in turns to share each of our experiences around the world. Although we're told we look similar, our personalities couldn't be further apart! Stefan is positive, impulsive, and outgoing, while Seby loves to carefully plan everything, is a bit more cautious and a true perfectionist. For us, this creates the perfect balance for a great holiday or trip away.

In this book, we have no agenda other than to share our experiences about our most memorable trips. We have not covered every destination in the world, so if something is not mentioned, it doesn't mean we don't rate it – we just haven't explored it enough yet!

We hope this book guides and inspires you to make the most of your adventures wherever they may be.

Stefan and Seby x

ABOUT US

Who is Seby and who is Stefan?

SEBASTIEN CHANEAC (AKA SEBY)

*B*onjour à tous! I'm Seby, originally from France, naturalized in the UK and now married to Stefan.

I am the computer geek behind Nomadic Boys. Stefan calls me "the Architect" because I do all the coding, SEO, and generally make sure that the site runs efficiently.

Since I was a young child, I've always had a passion for travelling. I was curious about other cultures, people, places, and foods. Growing up, I would spend hours watching travel documentaries on TV, following the stories of journalists going on crazy adventures around the world.

I, too, wanted to be an explorer. I, too, wanted to see the world!

The underwater world is my other passion: thanks to Jacques Cousteau, the famous French oceanographer. Through his documentaries, Cousteau brought the mysteries of the sea to millions in their living rooms. And I was one of them, glued to the screen. He inspired me to study marine biology and learn scuba diving.

I knew that one day, I would also dive in exotic places around the world.

Cooking is another hobby of mine. As a child, when I wasn't daydreaming about sea life, I would help my mother cook in the kitchen. There's something therapeutic about mixing ingredients together to create a delicious meal that brings joy to people.

I find it rewarding to discover a new place by tasting new foods. There is always a story behind every nation's dish, whether it dates back to an ancient practice or because it serves a practical purpose. Food connects us all, regardless of where we're from or what we believe in.

Since Stefan and I first met, travel was a central theme in our relationship. I remember my friends telling me that the real test in a relationship is whether you can survive one weekend travelling somewhere without killing each other! Well, in our case, we survived not just one trip, but several. As our relationship developed, we did longer trips, and we went further each time. Our first big holiday together was to Thailand in 2012. It was exciting because it was the furthest we'd ever been from home.

It was also exciting because on that trip to Thailand something happened to us, something momentous that changed our whole perspective of life: we decided there and then that not only were we truly meant for each other, but we also wanted to see the rest of the world together. The seeds of Nomadic Boys were sown.

Seby

Stefan

STEFAN ARESTIS

*A*nd I'm Stefan. The curly-haired Cypriot Londoner behind Nomadic Boys. I take care of all our travel-related content, our weekly newsletter, and social media on Nomadic Boys. Yes, that's me replying to every social media comment!

I'm also a travel nerd.

It all started when I was collecting stamps as a child. I would greedily harvest stamps from envelopes that friends and family would send me. Throughout the years, I connected with hundreds of fellow stamp collectors from all around the world, learning about their countries and cultures. That's where my passion for travel started.

> *I travelled whenever I got the opportunity. . . Travel gave me the courage and confidence to be myself.*

If I couldn't sound any more nerdy, I confess I'm also a HUGE Eurovision geek. I blame my family. We Cypriots LOVE to follow the Eurovision Song Contest and vote religiously (usually for Cyprus and Greece). So, every May, whilst I was growing up, we'd all gather and watch the Scandis, Soviet Bloc, and Balkan countries giving "douze points" to each other – the point is, thanks to Eurovision, I would dream of venturing to places like North Macedonia, Armenia, and Azerbaijan from a young age.

Today, I get all my travel inspiration from historical fiction. I love reading books like *Wolf of the Plains* by Conn Iggulden about the Genghis Khan dynasty or watching series like *Vikings* and *Marco Polo*.

Throughout my late teens and twenties, I travelled whenever I got the opportunity. This also coincided with me coming out as gay. Travel gave me the courage and confidence to be myself.

I met Seby in 2009. We instantly clicked.

"I want to discover the world!" he said to me on our first date at *Le Beaujolais* bar in Leicester Square. *"I'll go with you!"* I replied to the person who would become my life partner.

I've been to over 90 countries and would love to say I've covered the entire globe at some stage in my life.

I am happiest when I'm in a new place trying to negotiate my way around – ideally with my partner in crime, my Seby, to hand.

GAY TRAVEL 101

On the next few pages, we have collected all of the practical stuff that you need to think about before you travel as an openly queer person.

*F*or over a decade, we've been publishing online content about our experiences travelling the world as a gay couple. . . and, for some reason, people have lapped up every word. Millions read our content every year!

As much as we are humbled, we do pause and wonder: *Why do so many people from all around the world care to read about our travels*?

The answer is that the bulk of our readers are LGBTQ+ travellers looking to find out more information about the safety of that destination. For example, they want to know where they can stay without judgement, where they can go to meet like-minded people, and where the safe spaces are so that they can be affectionate with their partners.

Let us open the library real-quick (no, not *that* one, nobody's going to *read* you!): the word gay usually references gay men (and sometimes gay women) and LGBTQ+ (as well as "queer") refers to the wider community as a whole.

We have used these terms like so throughout this book.

Being gay means that we need to carry out this extra layer of groundwork before we can simply jet off anywhere. Since we both identify as gay men, the queer spaces we occupy tend to be gay male-focused – but not always! Our community is as diverse as it is vast: gay women, trans people, and other LGBTQ+ folk may have other considerations that they need to make before travelling, but we hope that the wider community still finds this book resourceful, useful, and most importantly, *fun*!

Our Gay Travel 101 includes all the indispensable lessons we've learnt that we think you need to be aware of. We are conscious that travelling in a place that is less gay-friendly than what you're used to can cause anxiety, so if you need somebody to talk to we recommend calling a trusted friend or an LGBTQ+ hotline, such as Switchboard.

→ WANT MORE NOMADIC BOYS TRAVEL WISDOM?

We've summarized all our trips to date here in this book, but readers can check out more stories and resources (including interviews with LGBTQ+ locals) on our blog nomadicboys.com. You can also find us on all social media channels as @nomadicboys

→Is it legal to be gay in the place I'm visiting?

Excited to visit Morocco?
See the pyramids in Egypt?
Party in downtown Beirut?
Bathe in the pristine turquoise waters of the Maldives?
Go on a safari in Sri Lanka?
Explore the rainforests of Borneo?

All of the above?

But can you guess what all these destinations have in common?

Every single one of these places has anti-gay laws. So, in theory, this means that the local police could arrest us if we were to simply walk the streets holding hands or do anything to show that we are openly gay. *Absolutely bonkers, right?!*

Many of our friends in some of these countries, say Malaysia or Sri Lanka, would say that these are just redundant laws that are never enforced – a hangover from the days of the British Empire and other colonial powers. In fact, before colonization, some indigenous cultures and countries did not discriminate against LGBTQ+ people at all!

However, the fact that these laws still exist today means we must be vigilant. Local police can use them as an excuse to harass LGBTQ+ people for a cash bribe as we found out in India (see pages 76–77). Unfortunately, these anti-LGBTQ+ laws also give licence to violent homophobic gangs to harass the LGBTQ+ community while local police turn a blind eye. Therefore, the first thing gay travellers need to check is: *Does the place you want to visit have any anti-LGBTQ+ laws?*

If yes, then you need to determine the extent to which you need to go back in the closet or, if you are uncomfortable with that, just skip that destination entirely (until laws and attitudes change).

→Is it safe to be openly gay?

Even if the place you want to visit doesn't have any anti-LGBTQ+ laws, it still may not be safe to be openly gay there. Countries like Russia and Turkey, eastern Europe, and even parts of the US – do not have anti-LGBTQ+ laws, but you would be putting your lives at risk if, say, you were to give your partner a quick peck on the cheek in public.

You need to know the extent to which society in these countries is socially conservative and how they feel about LGBTQ+ people so that you can refrain from doing anything that may put you in danger.

→Should you avoid PDAs?

Public displays of affection (PDAs) are something our straight friends take for granted: the brushing of an eyelash off your partner's cheek, dancing together, holding hands in public. . . for us, we have to be extra careful where we do this. We are generally quite conservative with PDAs and err on the side of caution unless we know we're in a

safe space. Despite the image we present online, we generally don't like drawing attention to ourselves – especially in public. That is why we seek out gay-friendly spaces where we know we will feel safe to fully express ourselves.

→Do you need a VPN to access the internet?

In a lot of places, the internet is heavily monitored, and various apps and websites are blocked. For example, Grindr is banned in Turkey, Lebanon, Indonesia, Qatar, and the UAE.

China takes this to a whole new level with an outright ban on not just Grindr, but almost every Western online entity including Instagram, Twitter, Dropbox, YouTube, Spotify, and all Google apps.

If you want to access these sites during your trip, then we recommend investing in a reputable VPN service on your device. A VPN will allow you to connect to the internet anonymously via another country's server, thereby bypassing local online restrictions.

Over the course of time, in many countries around the world, anti-LGBTQ+ laws tend to come and go. Openly gay hangouts and prides will shut down, and we learnt that in these situations, gay dating apps (like Grindr, Hornet, and Scruff) literally *become* the gay scene.

If you're travelling to countries with dubious anti-LGBTQ+ laws, a VPN will allow you to download these apps to connect with gay locals whether you're looking for a hookup or not (we weren't). But we quickly learnt how important these apps were in countries that have a hidden and underground gay scene, which wouldn't be visible to travellers after a Google search.

→Is it safe to post on your social media before and during your trip?

If you do choose to travel to a country with dubious LGBTQ+ laws and where the internet is strictly monitored, we strongly recommend that you avoid posting anything online before and during your trip.

We learnt this the hard way in Lebanon where a few innocuous Instagram posts with the #gaylebanon hashtag got us blacklisted and banned from ever being allowed to visit again (see pages 164–65)!

Another tip would be to consider setting your social media to private for the duration of your trip.

→Can you sleep with your partner in a double bed?

Sadly, this is something we always have to be mindful of whenever we are planning our trips.

In very obvious gay destinations like Fort Lauderdale, Key West, and Berlin, you know that most hotels welcome gay travellers. In fact, these destinations are likely to have a plethora of gay hotels that cater specifically to the LGBTQ+ community – some gay hotel chains like Axel even call themselves straight-friendly to emphasize this!

However, in destinations that aren't as gay-friendly, it pays to do more research. You need to find a hotel that you know will welcome gay couples and won't have an issue with two men wanting to share a bed.

Usually, the big brand names like Marriott, Hyatt, and Hilton are world famous for being gay-friendly wherever they are in the world. Others may publicly advertise that they are gay-friendly by stating this on their website or showing that they are affiliated to a gay travel organization, such as IGLTA. You can also find accommodation on the website *misterb&b*. It's the gay equivalent to Airbnb, and it only features gay-owned and gay-friendly accommodation.

Failing that, we recommend calling or emailing ahead to ask if they're okay to host a gay couple. Brace yourself: you'd be shocked at some of the horrific answers we've received from some hotels:

"No, we don't welcome that sort of thing in our hotel!"
"Ok, we can host you, but only if you avoid the public areas of the hotel as we have families with children also staying here."

Even though some of the conversations might be unpleasant, we feel you would rather have them over the phone or email than when you're already there, travel-weary and trying to check in!

→Is it safe to bring PrEP or HIV medication?

Most countries won't have an issue with the medication you carry. Some have strict rules about the amount of medication you bring and will only permit you to bring a specific quantity.

On the other hand, some places like Dubai require you to pre-register online any prescribed or over-the-counter medicines (including PrEP and HIV medication), and they will charge a hefty fine if you don't!

→Travelling solo or with a gay tour company?

We've experienced a mix of both solo trips and gay group trips. Both are fantastic.

For first time gay travellers who are quite anxious about vacationing solo, we recommend checking out some of the tours offered by reputable LGBTQ+ companies like Out Adventures, Detours, CODA Tours, Brand g Vacations, GaySail, HE Travel, Out Asia Travel, and Everything To Sea. Each one is owned and managed by LGBTQ+ people, offering a range of different trips.

→Make sure you have adequate travel insurance!

If there is one single piece of advice we can give, it's this!

If you need any emergency medical treatment, your iPhone is stolen, your luggage lost at the airport, your flights are cancelled. . . you'll be super thankful that you have insurance cover for it.

In any case, travel insurance policies are inexpensive, and the peace of mind they give us when things go wrong is invaluable.

→Where is the best place to visit for gay travellers?

Ah, the million-dollar question! Well, read on, dear reader, and we'll give you an insight into some of the places that have tickled and inspired us the most. . .

EUROPE

From Maspalomas Pride, Berlin's Folsom spectacle, *picture-perfect* Mykonos, the array of gay Mediterranean beaches, and the numerous queer winter ski festivals – Europe is *rife* with gayness. The continent is home to *the best* gay scenes, the best queer events, and the best gay nightlife you could dream of.

Naturally, we are biased – we've spent most of our time together exploring every nook and cranny our home continent has to offer, from *über gay* destinations like Gran Canaria and Sitges (both in Spain), to the more unexpected, like Georgia.

We're *proud* to have visited almost every single country in Europe, which has afforded us an overall impression of the continent's gay scene. In this section, we've selected some of our favourite and most *memorable stories* from our travel experiences in Europe.

↑ *Europe*

ENGLAND (LONDON)

The greatest city in the world. One of the most exciting places to live, with THE best gay scene you'll ever come across. FACT!

1 → FAVOURITE BRUNCH SPOT
Balans

2 → FAVOURITE GAY BAR IN SOHO
Comptons

3 → FAVOURITE BAR FOR A DRAG SHOW
Royal Vauxhall Tavern

4 → FAVOURITE GAY PARTY
Roast at Electrowerkz

5 → FAVOURITE GAY EVENT
London Pride

*A*dmittedly, we're totally biased. London was our home for a long time and the place where we met – back in February 2009 in Soho's G-A-Y. Setting aside our biases, London is truly a terrific city. It's eclectic – home to many different people from all around the world. There is always something to do here at any time of the day. The museums are grand, iconic, and most are free to enter. All of the world's best musicals, shows, and theatres feature on the West End.

And then there's the gay scene. *It's massive!*

London can be overwhelming for the first-timer. It's enormous, stressful, and let's face it, the grey weather doesn't help.

But it seems like almost every gay guy who visits ends up staying – just as Seby did as a shy, young twenty-something fresh from France, many, many moons ago. . .

LEFT Kissing with Pride on Regent Street.

OUR TOP EXPERIENCES

⬈ *London*

1 → PRIDE IN LONDON
Every June/July we join over a million revellers to sashay down the iconic streets of central London to celebrate our LGBTQ+ family. Interesting fact: it's officially called "Pride in London" to differentiate it from "London Pride" in London, Ontario in Canada! Check the Pride in London website for the latest info about the next event.

2 → GAY PUB CRAWL IN SOHO
This is the heart of London's gay scene, and is packed with awesome bars like Comptons, Village, Rupert Street Bar, G-A-Y, Ku Bar, the Admiral Duncan and many more.

3 → WATCH A WORLD-CLASS SHOW
Nothing beats watching the latest musical or show in London's West End theatres. They are world-famous!

4 → CABARETS AND DRAG SHOWS AT THE ROYAL VAUXHALL TAVERN
The RVT is an institution on the London gay scene featuring the best drag shows and cabaret performances every evening. Check the RVT website for details of the latest events and to book tickets. We recommend booking ahead as popular shows sell out quickly, especially at weekends.

5 → MIGHTY HOOPLA GAY MUSIC FESTIVAL
Every June we join 25,000 party goers for Mighty Hoopla at Brockwell Park in Brixton for a weekend of club nights, DJ sets, cabaret performances, hidden discos, and vogue competitions. Check the Hoopla website to find exact details of the next event, the full line up, and to buy tickets.

6 → POETRY NIGHTS AND POTTERY CLASSES AT THE COMMON PRESS
Walk along the cool Brick Lane in East London as you head to this LGBTQ+ multi-disciplinary venue for poetry nights, voguing classes, ballet classes, book launches, and self-care sessions. Check out the Common Press website for details of the next event and to buy tickets. We recommend booking ahead to avoid disappointment.

7 → SNAP A SELFIE ON CAMDEN'S RAINBOW CROSSING
Camden, home to Amy Winehouse and the world-famous market, now also has a permanent rainbow crossing at the junction of Jamestown Road and Hawley Crescent.

8 → GAY'S THE WORD BOOKSHOP AND WALK THE TRANS CROSSING
Further south from Camden, closer to Soho, on 66 Marchmont Street is the oldest LGBTQ+ bookshop in the UK called Gay's the Word. When you come outside and turn right, you'll see another permanent crossing, this time with the iconic blue, pink, and white colours of the transgender flag.

9 → QUEER BRITAIN MUSEUM AND COAL DROPS YARD
The area around King's Cross St. Pancras station has been completely transformed into a social hub with shops, canal-side drinking joints, landscaped green spaces, and is home to the UK's first dedicated national LGBTQ+ museum: the Queer Britain Museum. Entry is free although they occasionally have ticketed events like panel discussions and photography workshops, which you will need to book in advance.

10 → ROMANTIC WALK ALONG THE SOUTHBANK

Our favourite part of London. The Southbank lies across the river from Big Ben, and the London Eye is also found here. We love to walk along the river, taking in the most famous sites of the London skyline.

11 → TOWER OF LONDON & TOWER BRIDGE

Tower Bridge is one of the most recognizable sites of London, and the Tower of London lies next to it. This is where the famous Crown Jewels are kept! Check out the Queer Lives tour during LGBTQ+ History Month every February.

Seby

"I'M GOING TO MARRY THAT GUY ONE DAY"

↗ *London*

. . . I proclaimed to my best friend Johan when I first laid eyes on Him.

*I*t was the height of summer 2007. Like every Saturday evening, Johan and I would hit the gay bars of Soho's Old Compton Street, the heart of London's gay scene. We started our night at Village for some karaoke then headed to Comptons bar to flirt with the daddies (who bought us a few drinks). Then we ended up at the G-A-Y Late Club where we danced till the early hours. All the pretty boys came here!

As soon as we entered G-A-Y my eyes were drawn to this hot Greek-looking guy dancing topless on the dancefloor.

I could not take my eyes off him! I grabbed Johan. . .

"Johan, Johan, look! You see that guy over there? Him, over there. One day I'm going to marry Him, but he doesn't know it yet!"

And he wouldn't know it for another few years: I was too shy to go over and say hi. *What if he doesn't like me? What if he's got a boyfriend? What if. . .* The fear of rejection got a hold of me. He was dancing with his friends and didn't

see me. We went to the bar to grab a few drinks but when we returned to the dancefloor He had disappeared.

I didn't see Him again, but I knew I would never forget Him – my mysterious, handsome stranger who had just pierced my heart with the arrow of love. *And he had no idea.*

The next day, Johan slammed a copy of the latest QX Magazine (one of the free weekly gay magazines in London) on my desk. On the front cover was a really hot guy dressed in a skimpy football outfit modelling for a new sports fetish gay party at Central Station – a gay bar in King's Cross famous for its themed parties. IT WAS HIM! And oh-my-GOD, he looked HOT!

Johan grinned at me and jokingly said: *"That guy from yesterday? That's him right there on the front cover! Dream on Seby, you'll never have him!"*

We both laughed, but deep down I knew that somehow, some day, we would meet again. Two years later, Johan and I were in the same gay bar. We were tipsy, giggling, gossiping, watching all the pretty boys come and go.

Suddenly, from the corner of my eye, I spotted Him.

"Johan, look! It's Him – the guy I told you I was going to marry. Remember? From two years ago? He was on the front cover of QX in his football kit. . . He is right there!"

This time He noticed me. He was deep in conversation with his friend, but every so often he would glance at me. Our eyes would lock, and for a moment, time would stop! He would then smile at me.

Oh, that smile – how it made me melt!

"Go and talk to Him Seby! Just say hello

Maybe Johan was right, how on earth could I realistically believe that I could ever get with a guy like Him?

That toxic thought was quickly burst by His friend who came over to me and handed me a piece of paper.

"Hi, my friend really likes you but he's too shy to come over, so here's his number. Please can I give him yours?"

Words cannot describe how I felt. I was elated. My heart was RACING – it was the most exciting moment of my life! I quickly scribbled down my number and gave it to his friend. I felt like I was walking on Cloud 9. . .

A few days later I had my first date

He would glance at me every so often. Our eyes would lock, and for a moment, time would stop!

---

and ask where He is from," said Johan.

Despite Johan's encouragement I was transfixed, frozen to the spot. My legs refused to move.

After a few drinks I plucked up the courage to go over to Him. I got close and managed to whisper, *"Bonjour!"* but got so scared that I quickly ran away to the bar.

I blew it!

I re-joined Johan feeling silly and glum.

The evening in G-A-Y progressed but despite my failed attempt to communicate, He continued to look over at me, each time smiling, each time causing the ground to tremble beneath me! Neither of us spoke to each other. He was also shy.

After a while He put on his coat and began to leave. *"Not again!"* I thought.

with Him. It was Friday the 27th of February, 2009. I took Him to *Le Beaujolais*, a French bar I love in Leicester Square.

His name was Stefan. He was Greek Cypriot, born and raised in London. He was also *irresistibly* charming (*and still is!*). I was besotted with him!

Very quickly into our date I told him that I had always dreamed of travelling the world. At this point he took my hand and said to me with the sweetest smile, *"I would love that too"*.

And so, we did!

Fast-forward to June 2018 when we got legally married at Ealing Town Hall in West London, I turned to my best friend, Johan, and with a great big smile on my face I proudly declared: *"I told you I would marry that guy!"*

✦ Europe

FRANCE

*"**The greatest country in the world**!"* proclaims Seby every morning as he gets ready to leave our house to buy us a couple of fresh baguettes from a local boulangerie. . .

**1 → FAVOURITE
PARIS DISTRICT**
Le Marais

**2 → FAVOURITE GAY
BAR FOR A COCKTAIL**
Cox, Paris

**3 → FAVOURITE SKI
RESORT**
Les Arcs, Savoie

**4 → FAVOURITE
GAY PARTY**
Lou Queernaval, Nice

**5 → FAVOURITE
CYCLE ROUTE**
Lavender fields,
Provence

*I*t is his Motherland after all, but there is good reason why France is one of the most visited places in the world. From culturally rich UNESCO-listed sites to world-class cuisine, beautiful beaches, stunning mountain scenery, and smoking-hot lovers. . . France really has it all!

Also, France is, historically, very gay. They've paved the way forward centuries in advance by legalizing homosexuality way back in 1791. The French have long held a belief in "laissez-faire" towards same-gender relationships; in other words, not interfering in matters that may seem too personal and respecting the privacy of others.

We definitely feel tolerance and acceptance when we're around French people. Most of the French don't bat an eyelid when we come out to them. We have never experienced homophobia in France. However, there are many suburbs where homophobia is rife but as a tourist, you're unlikely to ever need to go to there.

When it comes to the gay scene, Paris leads the way with Le Marais – a gorgeous district of the French capital full of cutesy gay cafes, bars, parties, and other LGBTQ+ businesses. Most of the other big cities, such as Nice, Marseille, Lyon, Lille, and Montpellier, have thriving gay scenes.

We love France just as much as France loves us!

LEFT The iconic Eiffel Tower.

OUR TOP EXPERIENCES
✈ *France*

1 → EXPLORING PARIS

The main sites of Paris are within walking distance of each other. The Eiffel Tower is the most famous attraction, which many visit to propose to their partner. Our favourite walk in Paris is from Arc de Triomphe to the Louvre Museum along the world-famous Champs-Élysées avenue.

2 → DISNEYLAND PARIS PRIDE

Every year in June, Disneyland Paris hosts Magical Pride. For a weekend, Disneyland becomes even more magical with rainbows everywhere, special shows, and an evening party when the park stays open until 2a.m.

3 → LE MARAIS IN PARIS

Our favourite district in Paris is like stepping into another age, with its narrow cobblestone streets, tight crowded cafes, and hidden courtyards. Le Marais is also the heart of the Parisian gay scene with gay bars like Cox, Cactus, El Hombre, and Bears' Den.

4 → EUROPEAN SNOW PRIDE

One of the best gay ski events in the world. It takes place over a week in March in a small French ski resort town in the Alps. Les Arcs, Les Menuires, Tignes, Avoriaz, and L'Alpe d'Huez have all hosted. People, from complete beginners (like Stefan) to advanced pro skiers (like Seby), come from all over to attend.

5 → LOU QUEERNAVAL

The Lou Queernaval is the LGBTQ+ segment of the world-famous Nice Carnival that takes place every February. One day is allocated during the Carnival to this gay carnival. It is extravagant, flamboyant, and really fun!

6 → PARIS GAY PRIDE

The Marche des Fiertés LGBT in Paris is the biggest gay event in France, which usually takes place on the last Sunday in June. The parade starts at Tour Montparnasse and culminates at Place de la Bastille. We love the atmosphere in Le Marais after Paris Pride – it's like one big gay summer carnival!

7 → LYON LIGHT FESTIVAL

The Fête des Lumières takes place over four nights around 8th December each year in Lyon. It honours Mary, mother of Jesus, who allegedly saved the city from a terrible plague in 1643. During the festival, residents place candles outside their windows and there are dramatic light displays on the buildings of the city. Lyon is beautiful at the best of times, but during the Light Festival it's truly magical!

8 → PICNIC AT VERSAILLES

On one road trip we visited the Palace of Versailles built by Louis XIV in 1682. It is giving "Opulence! You own everything!" It is surrounded by beautiful, landscaped gardens and parks. Picnics are allowed in the park, especially on the Saint Anthony Plain, between the Palace and the Trianon.

09

9 → CANOEING ON THE ARDÈCHE RIVER

The Ardèche region in southeast France, where Seby's father is from, is famous for its chestnuts. It is nicknamed "France's nature playground" because of its stunning gorges, rivers, waterfalls, and mountains. The best way to take it all in is to rent a canoe and paddle along the Ardèche River. Lyon is the closest airport hub city for Ardèche. The main town for the region where trains go to is called Lavilledieu.

10 → CYCLING THROUGH THE LAVENDER FIELDS OF PROVENCE

When they are in bloom in July, there's nothing more romantic than wading through the lavender fields of Provence. The Valensole Plateau's lavender fields are the most popular, but we prefer to rent bikes and cycle through the less well-known fields near Sault village. The main airport hubs for Provence are Avignon and Nîmes. The closest major train station is in the city of Aix-en-Provence.

THE NETHERLANDS (AMSTERDAM)

We've been travelling to the Dutch capital for many years, for weekend city breaks or specific gay events like Amsterdam Pride in August – it always leaves us gagging for more!

1 → FAVOURITE GAY BAR
SoHo Amsterdam

2 → FAVOURITE BAR FOR A DRAG SHOW
Lellebel

3 → FAVOURITE GAY PARTY
Club ChUrch

4 → FAVOURITE GAY EVENT
Amsterdam Pride in August

5 → FAVOURITE MUSIC EVENT
Milkshake Festival in July/August

*T*olerance is a way of life here! The Dutch are a remarkably open-minded bunch who have long embraced the LGBTQ+ community. Notably, the Netherlands made history by becoming the first nation in the world to legalize gay marriage back in 2001.

We experience a rare sense of ease in Amsterdam, where walking the streets holding hands feels completely natural without the need to constantly glance over our shoulders to gauge our safety.

Beyond its large gay scene, Amsterdam boasts a distinct urban landscape featuring 165 canals, more than 1,200 bridges, and a myriad of charming, narrow cobblestone streets. The city's picturesque beauty is so captivating that the 17th-century historic old town (called the Canal Ring) earned recognition as a UNESCO World Heritage Site in 2010.

And have we mentioned the infamous coffeeshops?

~~~~~~~~~~~~

RIGHT "You don't need a bicycle when you've got a Stefan to carry you through Amsterdam!"

OUR TOP EXPERIENCES

✈ *Amsterdam*

1 → THE GAY BARS ON REGULIERSDWARSSTRAAT

This is the heart of the Amsterdam gay scene with bars like SoHo Amsterdam (*not to be confused with the nearby Soho House!*), Bar Blend, Cafe Reality, and clubs like NYX. The best lesbian bar on the street is Café B'Femme. A pub crawl here is a must, especially during the summer months.

2 → AMSTERDAM PRIDE ON THE CANALS IN AUGUST

The only gay Pride event that takes place on water with around 80 boat floats that snake their way through the iconic canals. The Canal Parade is part of Pride Amsterdam, which also includes street parties, cultural events, and scandalous after-parties hosted by queer circuit party Rapido.

3 → MILKSHAKE FESTIVAL

A two-day open air music festival that celebrates diversity. It takes place every summer in Westerpark, usually in late July/early August just before Amsterdam Pride. It features famous local and international acts and attracts around 25,000 people each day.

4 → TULIPS OF AMSTERDAM

The Tulip Season runs from the end of March to mid-May, and the flowers are in full bloom in April. The best place to see them is at Keukenhof located in the small town of Lisse, around 30 miles southwest of Amsterdam. Some fields are even multi-coloured, creating a sickening rainbow effect!

5 → KING'S DAY (KONINGSDAG)

The King's birthday on 27th April is a national holiday in the Netherlands. The gay venues on Reguliersdwarsstraat all converge to create a carnival-like street party, becoming the second-largest outdoor gay party in the Netherlands (after Amsterdam Pride).

6 → TROPIKALI FESTIVAL IN JUNE

One of the best LGBTQ+ music festivals in the Netherlands that takes place every June in North Amsterdam. It features music from all around the world.

7 → ANNE FRANK HOUSE

A must for all. This is the house where Anne Frank and her family hid from the Nazis inside The Secret Annex. It's harrowing, but unforgettable.

8 → TRY A SPACE CAKE IN A COFFEESHOP

Marijuana is legal for personal use in the Netherlands and these coffeeshops sell brownies (space cakes) that are infused with cannabis. However, please take care,

→ WORLDPRIDE 2026

Amsterdam will be Ground Zero for the gays in 2026. The Netherlands is going to go ALL OUT to make this the best gay event the world has ever seen! Amsterdam is no stranger to hosting big gay events – it hosted EuroPride twice: in 1994 and in 2016.

especially if this is your first time. The marijuana sold is pure and therefore strong, so go easy otherwise you'll be sashaying away early before the night's even begun!

9 → CRUISE ON THE CANALS

The canals are one of the most iconic things about Amsterdam. There are many companies that will let you rent out canal boats for an agreed time slot. During the summer months, we love grabbing a few drinks with our best Judies and hiring out a boat for half a day. Some boat owners even rent out their boats to stay in, usually listed in sites like misterb&b, Booking.com, and Airbnb.

10 → AMSTERDAM LIGHT FESTIVAL

Takes place annually from late November until mid-January. The streets and buildings inside the Canal Ring are lit up with spectacular light sculptures and projections.

11 → RED LIGHT SECRETS MUSEUM

The world's first museum of sex work located in a former brothel in the Red Light District. It's one of the most fascinating museums we've ever been to! As part of the museum tour, you get the chance to sit behind one of the windows to see what it's like being watched from the streets. Get ready to *serve*, heeny!

"MY EMBARRASSING SECRET"

✦ *Amsterdam*

Ready to go on our bikes, it was time for my confession. . .

"What do you mean you never came off stabilizers, Stefan?!" Seby was utterly flabbergasted when I confessed to him that I never properly learnt how to ride a bike. It was in the early years of our relationship as we embarked on our first cycling holiday together in the Netherlands.

Seby was bubbling with excitement because every weekend growing up, he would cycle through the beautiful French countryside with his family, and he was eager to share this cherished passion with me. But for me, growing up in the concrete jungle of suburban North London, my biking experiences were limited to going around the neighbourhood a few times on a bike supported with stabilizers.

Despite my lack of experience, I was determined to make our trip perfect. I wanted to impress Seby, so I decided not to tell him about my inability to ride a bike.

As we set off on our rental bikes in downtown Amsterdam, I put on a brave face, thinking, *"I can wing this, I don't need to say anything to Seby. People cycle all the time: how hard can this really be?"*

However, my secret was exposed the moment I attempted to pedal along a quaint street close to the picturesque Brouwersgracht (Brewer's Canal). In no time, I lost my balance and took a tumble, narrowly avoiding falling into the water.

Seby rushed over to me, concerned, and cried out, *"Stefan! What just happened? Are you okay?!"*

That was the moment I came clean about my cycling. . .

"STEFAN! How can you, a 30-year-old man, not know how to ride a bike? Are you serious?!"

Despite his initial shock, Seby was amazing about it. He helped me back up on the bike, holding onto me as I

My secret was exposed the moment I attempted to pedal along a quaint street close to the picturesque Brouwersgracht!

attempted to cycle once again. With his support, I managed to go a bit further, but as soon as he let go, I lost my balance and fell.

We tried again. And again. Gradually, with each attempt, I gained more confidence and found my balance, allowing us to venture into more populated areas.

Seby later admitted that he was secretly terrified as he watched me cycle in front of him, seemingly confident, but with my bike swaying from side to side, as if I were about to tumble over.

He needn't have worried! Biking in Amsterdam is perfect for beginners. The city is flat, bike lanes are ubiquitous, and with almost everyone on two wheels, there are few cars to worry about.

Biking around the Dutch capital on our bikes felt incredibly liberating! Throughout the rest of our holiday, we explored different parts of the city and my cycling confidence grew with each ride. By the end of the trip, I had transformed from a complete cycling novice to an enthusiast. Upon returning to London, I purchased a Trek road bike, and now proudly cycle everywhere.

↑ Europe

SPAIN

Spain has been our go-to travel destination for years, ranking as one of our top gay hotspots in the world.

1 → FAVOURITE GAY PRIDE EVENT
Madrid Pride in June/July

2 → FAVOURITE GAY PARTY/FESTIVAL
Bear Week in Sitges

3 → FAVOURITE GAY SCENE
Maspalomas in Gran Canaria

4 → FAVOURITE GAY BEACH
Mar Bella in Barcelona

5 → FAVOURITE ROAD TRIP
Andalusia; including stopovers in Granada, Córdoba, Seville, and Grazalema

LEFT Gaudí's Casa Battló lit up in full glory for the Barcelona Pride festival.

*B*arcelona holds a special place in our hearts – an artistic city adorned with beautiful beaches right at its doorstep and a thriving gay scene in the Eixample area (often nicknamed Gaixample – a combination of the Catalan word for gay, *gai*, and Eixample, the district's name). Spain's captivating beauty is another reason why we keep going back. Our favourite region is Andalusia, the enchanting southern part of the country, deeply rooted in flamenco culture. Then there's all the many gay beaches of Spain, most of which are clothing optional.

"You go first, Stefan. I'll remove my Speedos after you've taken off yours!"

We'll never forget those first tentative moments on the Playa del Muerto gay naked beach of Sitges. It was our first time at a nudist area, so we were shy. However, once we overcame our initial hesitations, a strong sense of liberation washed over us! Just letting it all hang out in the sunshine, freely swimming in the Mediterranean Sea with nothing to conceal – it was an indescribable feeling!

And then there's the food – paellas, tapas, jamón, chorizo, gazpacho, churros, tortillas, and the world-famous La Rioja wine. For the adventurous foodies, we dare you to try *oreja de cerdo* (pig's ears), a speciality of Madrid!

Spain is a top gay destination that just keeps on giving!

OUR TOP EXPERIENCES

✈ *Spain*

1 → THE GAY SCENE OF MADRID
The Chueca district is the beating gay heart and soul of the city with gay hangouts like D'Mystic, LaKama, and LL Bar. The city blows up in early July when over 2 million people descend here for Madrid Pride – the largest gay Pride in Europe and second largest in the world after São Paulo. Madrid is also a cultural hub with world-class art museums like Reina Sofia and the Prado. She fancy!

2 → THE GAY SCENE OF BARCELONA
The city has stunning beaches, including the clothing-optional Mar Bella gay beach. The vibrant Gaixample area is home to hotspots like Moeem, Priscilla Cafe, Punto, Museum Bar, and La Sastrería. Top gay events we recommend checking out in Barcelona include Pride in June and the party-packed Circuit Festival in August.

3 → GET CULTURAL IN BARCELONA
If you're a culture queen, Barcelona is brimming with cultural delights. We love marvelling at Gaudí's architectural masterpieces, especially the iconic Sagrada Familia. Getting lost in the enchanting Gothic Quarter's medieval narrow streets is another favourite pastime. Other recommendations include the Picasso Museum, Park Güell, and the gorge views from Montjuïc hill.

4 → THE GAY MECCA OF GRAN CANARIA
There is an entire gay shopping centre here called Yumbo Centre; we love Mardi Gras for drinks and Mantrix for dancing. Gay-friendly hotels include AxelBeach Maspalomas and there is a clothing-optional gay beach located a 15 minutes walk through the infamous sand dunes (which is also a notorious cruising area!). Don't miss the best events: Bear Carnival in March, Maspalomas Pride in May, Maspalomas Fetish Week in October, and Winter Pride in November.

5 → RELAX IN SITGES
A small gay seaside town, with a fun gay scene centred around Parrots Pub. Our favourite nudist beaches are Playa de los Balmins and Playa del Muerto. The town hosts several LGBTQ+ annual events including Carnival in February, Bear Week1 in April/May, Gay Pride Sitges in June, and Bear Week2 in September.

6 → PARTY HARD IN IBIZA
Although renowned for its legendary parties, with mega clubs like Pacha accommodating up to 3,000 people, Ibiza's

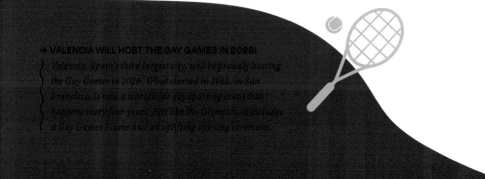

→ VALENCIA WILL HOST THE GAY GAMES IN 2026!
Valencia, Spain's third largest city, will be proudly hosting the Gay Games in 2026. What started in 1982, in San Francisco, is now a worldwide gay sporting event that happens every four years. Just like the Olympics, it includes a Gay Games Flame and an uplifting opening ceremony.

04

old town is particularly charming and hosts a small gay scene in the Calle de la Virgen neighbourhood. Be sure to check out Bar 22, Lady D., MAD Bar, DADO, Sunrise Ibiza, and JJ Bar. There's also the Es Cavallet gay beach.

7 → ROAD TRIP IN ANDALUSIA

One of the most rewarding holidays we've ever done together. This region is full of architectural wonders such as the Alcázar palace of Seville, the Mesquita-Catedral of Córdoba, and the grand UNESCO-listed Alhambra palace of Granada. The region is also a joy for hiking – our favourite was around the charming village of Grazalema in Cádiz.

8 → CATCH THE SUN IN TORREMOLINOS

A former humble fishing village along the Costa del Sol, the La Nogalera area is where the main gay hangouts can be found, including Pourquoi Pas?, Eden Beach Club, and Discoteca Parthenon. Torremolinos Pride takes place annually in May/June.

9 → GAYCATION IN BENIDORM

Another popular seaside resort town – largely thanks to the success of Benidorm Pride in September, which has grown to become one of the most popular annual queer events in Spain. The Benidorm Old Town features a few gay hangouts including Sensations, Company Bar, and Gspot.

GEORGIA

Georgia surprised us at every turn with its unspoiled beauty, rich cultural heritage, and landscapes like something out of a fairy tale.

1 → FAVOURITE GAY PARTY
Horoom Nights at Bassiani club, Tbilisi

2 → FAVOURITE GAY BAR
Success Bar, Tbilisi

3 → FAVOURITE FOOD
Khachapuri

4 → FAVOURITE TREK
Kazbegi region

5 → FAVOURITE TOUR
Wine tasting in the Kakheti region

We knew nothing about Georgia before our visit, so admittedly we came here not knowing what to expect. One thing that we were delighted to discover was that Georgia is a foodie's paradise! The Georgian cuisine is DIVINE with mouth-watering highlights like *khinkali* (Georgian dumplings), *khachapuri* (Georgian cheese bread), *chkmeruli* (fried chicken doused in a scrumptious creamy garlic sauce), and Stefan's personal favourite – *badrijani nigvzit* (fried aubergines stuffed with walnut, garlic, and topped with pomegranate). As Latrice Royale would say: *eat it!* And with an 8,000-year history of wine production, Georgia also offers exciting wines to try.

When it comes to gay life in Georgia, society is conservative. Life for LGBTQ+ locals is not easy. Homophobia is common. The unyielding Face Control entry policy outside most queer venues is a stark reminder of this (see pages 44–45). Despite this, we were pleasantly surprised to find a bustling gay scene in Tbilisi with several queer venues, including the largest gay party in the Caucasus called Horoom Nights.

OUR TOP EXPERIENCES

1 → THE GAY SCENE OF TBILISI
The Tbilisi gay scene is based mainly around the Rustaveli area (just north of the old town) and includes queer venues like Success Bar, Unholy Bar, Ambavi, and clubs like KHIDI and Cafe Gallery.

2 → WANDERING IN TBILISI'S OLD TOWN
We loved winding our way through the little side streets of Tbilisi's old town, also known as Abanotubani. It has a unique otherworldly charm, making you feel cut off from the rest of the world. Unique sites to look out for include the Narikala Fortress, the Bridge of Peace, Freedom Square, and the sulfur bathhouses.

3 → TREKKING IN KAZBEGI
Our standout highlight from our trip! The Kazbegi region in northeast Georgia is surrounded with stunning mountains. The region is famous for its view from the Tsminda Sameba Church (also known as the Gergeti Trinity Church). The trek reaches an altitude up to 2,200m (7,218ft)!

4 → THE ANANURI CASTLE COMPLEX
Conveniently located on the road between Tbilisi and Kazbegi. This is a UNESCO World Heritage site that was the scene of countless feuds and battles throughout Georgia's history. Views from the castle's towers offer a stunning view of the Arkala River, which sparkles under the sun.

5 → WINE TASTING IN THE KAKHETI REGION
The Kakheti province in the east is the main wine-producing area, and houses the best wineries such as Chateau Mere, Winery Khareba, and Chateau Mukhrani. *Salut!*

6 → VISITING THE DAVID GAREJA MONASTERY COMPLEX
Also located in the Kakheti region, this monastery was built in the 6th century, and straddles the border between Georgia and Azerbaijan. The best way to visit it is on a 2-hour day trip from Tbilisi.

7 → THE ANCIENT CAVE CITY OF VARDZIA
Built in the 1100s under the Erusheli Mountain, it was an underground sanctuary from invading Mongols. It takes around 5 hours to reach Vardzia from Tbilisi by bus, so best done as part of a tour rather than a day trip.

8 → GEORGIA'S FORMER CAPITAL OF MTSKHETA
One of the oldest cities in Georgia, Mtskheta is regarded as the birthplace of Christianity in Georgia. The 11th-century Svetitskhoveli Cathedral is thought to be the burial site of Jesus Christ's robes. Mtskheta is around 15 miles north of Tbilisi, so easy to reach by taxi or public transport.

9 → UPLISTSIKHE CAVE TOWN FORTRESS
One of the oldest urban settlements in the area, some structures date back to the Iron Age. It consists of several hundred rooms that have been impressively carved into a cliff. Uplistsikhe was once a lively trading town on the Silk Road and is located 80km (50 miles) west of Tbilisi, taking around 1.5 hours to reach.

Georgia is a foodie's paradise! The cuisine is *divine*, with mouth-watering highlights like *khinkali, khachapuri, chkmeruli,* and *badrijani nigvzit.* As Latrice Royale would say: *eat it*!

OUR PRACTICAL TIPS FOR LGBTQ+ TRAVELLERS

✈ *Georgia*

1 → REMAIN CAUTIOUS WITH PDAS

Although homosexuality is legal in Georgia, unfortunately you should avoid public displays of affection unless you're in a queer-friendly space. Older members of Georgian society are socially conservative and frown on LGBTQ+ lifestyles. We didn't encounter any problems during our time in Georgia, but equally we didn't openly display that we were a couple in public.

2 → GAY-FRIENDLY HOTELS

Despite being such a socially conservative and religious country, surprisingly we had few problems finding a hotel that would accommodate us (unlike other East European countries we visited). Every international hotel told us they welcome LGBTQ+ travellers. We stayed at the following hotels in Tbilisi, which we can confirm are welcoming to gay couples (as of print): the Vinotel Boutique Hotel, Courtyard by Marriott Tbilisi, and Fabrika Hostel.

3 → CHECK TRAVEL ADVICE

Check your government's foreign office website before you go and avoid the self-proclaimed breakaway regions of South Ossetia and Abkhazia.

RIGHT A fabulous trek through the Kazbegi mountains in Georgia!

FEIS KONTROL

➤ *Georgia*

We had to pass Face Control before entering Horoom Nights!

"*Will he let us in Seby?! We followed all their online instructions so it should be ok, right? Do we smile at him? Should we camp it up a bit and hold hands? Or just stand next to each other, subdued, avoiding all eye contact with anyone?*"

We had heard so much about Horoom Nights – an extraordinary queer techno party at the famed Bassiani club in Tbilisi, hailed as "the largest gay party in the Caucasus", accommodating up to 1,200 revellers.

So of course, we had to check it out. However, you can't just turn up and expect to be let in.

We first had to create profiles on the Bassiani.com website and undergo verification. The process demanded an array of personal details, including our passport numbers and social media profiles.

Seby grumbled throughout the application process, questioning the need to divulge so much personal information just to attend a gay club.

I reminded him that these stringent measures were in place to ensure our safety. Georgia has a history of homophobic violence, and the Bassiani club aimed to protect the LGBTQ+ community by filtering out potential threats. Any overt homophobia on our social media profiles would be picked up on and our applications automatically rejected. Understanding the rationale, Seby forgave the intrusive bureaucracy.

After a few days we received a notification confirming our verified accounts, granting us the privilege to pre-order tickets for the upcoming Horoom Nights party. I felt so excited receiving that email: it was like we were gay superheroes being admitted into this exclusive underground VIP club!

Yet, having a ticket did not guarantee us entry. We still had to pass the infamous *Feis Kontrol* – a Soviet hangover where the bouncer's snap decision determined our fate. . .

"*We're next in the queue, Seby. Let's agree to keep a neutral expression,* don't smile, and just act cool. We got this!"

The moment of truth arrived.

The imposing bouncer, his stoic gaze unwavering, scrutinized us from head to toe.

Eventually he nodded, turned round to open the door, granting us passage.

Well, until a second bouncer stopped us and asked for our phones. We gave them to him, and he put a sticker over the cameras to cover them.

We wondered what on earth we were going to encounter in Bassiani that required such secrecy!

He then told us to read and agree to their rules for entry – kind of like Tyler Durden's *"The first rule of Fight Club is that you do not talk about Fight Club!"*

signs, but the hypnotic throb of techno music acted as our North Star, guiding us to the dancefloor.

The atmosphere was electric, charged with a palpable sense of liberation and raw energy. The air was infused with the heat of topless bodies all around us moving to the rhythm of techno. *You could cut the sexual tension with a knife!*

From the corner of my eye, I saw two topless guys who had been making out on the dancefloor head to another room, which was pitch-black save for some subtle lighting – the darkroom.

Our Georgian friend, Giorgi, explained to us:

"Most guys here live with their homophobic families in small Soviet-style apartment blocks so they can

---

The atmosphere was electric, charged with a palpable sense of liberation and raw energy.

The Bassiani rules were not quite on that level. These rules are in place to safeguard the anonymity of patrons.

Entering Bassiani felt like we were in a post-apocalyptic Berlin-style underground club. We passed through a labyrinth of concrete rooms and dimly lit corridors, descending deeper into the enigmatic space. There were no guiding

never host a Grindr date. Bassiani is one of the few safe spaces where they can come and make out freely with their partner without fearing any repercussions."

We continued dancing to the techno beats that Bassiani club is so renowned for, losing track of time as the night unfolded.

GERMANY (BERLIN)

We always have a fun time when we visit Berlin – often lauded as the gay capital of Europe.

1 → MOST MEMORABLE EXPERIENCE
Getting into Berghain

2 → FAVOURITE GAY BAR
Heile Welt

3 → TOP GAY EVENT
Berlin Pride

4 → MOST POPULAR FETISH EVENT
Folsom Europe

5 → FAVOURITE FOOD
Currywurst German sausage (oh matron!)

A gay night out in Berlin is an experience in its own right, especially Berghain. It's so iconic that "Berlin-style club" has become a well-worn phrase used by similar clubs from Tel Aviv to Bangkok to describe their vibe.

And what *is* that vibe? Imagine a cavernous, dimly-lit former industrial warehouse, throbbing with electro house and techno. Strict "no photo" rules. Everyone dressed in all-black. Edgy. Gritty. Obligatory darkroom. Totally sex positive. *You get the gist*.

We must stress that not every gay club in Berlin is like this. We are humble, Britney pop-loving gay guys who just want to boogie to the likes of Spice Girls, Madonna, Lady Gaga, Beyoncé, Katy Perry. . . For that, SchwuZ club in the Neukölln borough fits the bill nicely.

Beyond all the wild sex-fuelled parties, Berlin is also a beacon of culture, with 170 museums, 440 galleries, three UNESCO World Heritage Sites, and a unique history that dates back to the 1200s.

→ SCHÖNEBERG: WORLD'S FIRST GAY VILLAGE

In 1896, the world's first gay magazine, Der Eigene, was created. By 1897, the world's first ever LGBTQ+ organization, the Scientific-Humanitarian Committee, was established, and they fervently lobbied the German government for equal rights. In 1919, the German movie Different From The Others became the first to positively portray homosexuality, and in 1922, the first ever gay demonstration took place in Nollendorfplatz, Schöneberg. These groundbreaking events set the stage for Berlin's rise as a vibrant gay capital, culminating in the world's first ever Gay Village in Schöneberg in the 1920s. At its zenith, it boasted around 40 queer venues including the famed Eldorado cabaret bar where Marlene Dietrich performed.

BELOW The iconic Brandenburg
Gate lit up with Pride.

OUR TOP EXPERIENCES
✈ *Berlin*

1 → THE GAY SCENE OF BERLIN
Since the 1920s, Schöneberg has been the beating heart of Berlin's LGBTQ+ community with bars like WOOF, Tom's Bar, Hafen, Heile Welt, and Prinzknecht. However, most young, hip gay Berliners we met coaxed us over to other neighbourhoods such as Kreuzberg (home to Möbel Olfe and Roses), Neukölln (where you'll find SchwuZ, Silverfuture, and Cocktail d'Amore), and Friedrichshain (known for Pornceptual, Bar Zum schmutzigen Hobby, Berghain, and Buttons).

2 → TRY TO GET INTO THE EXCLUSIVE BERGHAIN!
Berghain is one of the largest gay clubs in the world, housed in a former power plant spread across three floors. The parties here are legendary, stretching from Friday evening to deep into Monday morning. The queue to get in is just as epic, as are the bouncers who will reject you if they don't like your look. Even Britney was rumoured to have been denied entry! Our advice to get in: wear all black, don't smile, avoid going as a big group, and try to go on a Sunday lunchtime when it's less busy.

3 → PARTY AT BERLIN PRIDE IN JULY
Berlin Pride is one of Europe's best LGBTQ+ events, drawing in around 1 million people. The highlight is the Saturday parade that snakes its way through the city, culminating at Brandenburg Gate. In Germany, gay Pride events are aptly named Christopher Street Day, paying homage to the historic Stonewall Inn's location in New York.

4 → GO ON A GAY WALKING TOUR
We did a gay walking tour with Dr Finn Ballard (www.finn-ballard-tours.com), who we cannot recommend enough. As well as being knowledgeable about the LGBTQ+ history of Berlin, Finn also gave us a heart-warming and inspiring account of his own journey as a trans man. He shed light on the vibrant trans community in Berlin, making our tour not just educational but also profoundly moving.

5 → GET KINKY AT FOLSOM EUROPE
The largest fetish festival in Europe, going strong since 2003. It's the cousin of San Francisco's equivalent Folsom event, and attracts over 20,000 guys who are into a range of fetishes. The crown jewel of Folsom Europe is the outdoor Folsom Europe Street Fair, a vibrant extravaganza. Other famous fetish events in Berlin include Easter Berlin Leather Fetish Week in March/April and the electrifying HustlaBall in October.

6 → VISIT THE SCHWULES MUSEUM
Located in Schöneberg, the Schwules Museum is dedicated to the history and culture of the LGBTQ+ community. Established in 1985, it is now the world's largest institution for the queer community with over 50,000 artifacts that illuminate the tapestry of gay culture from vintage postcards to eclectic clothing and vinyl records. It's open almost every day (except Tuesdays).

7 → INDULGE IN A ROMANTIC SUNSET DINNER AT THE BERLIN TV TOWER
Standing 368m (1207ft) in the air, the Fernsehturm (TV Tower) is a globally recognized landmark that forms a prominent fixture on the city's skyline. It has a viewing gallery and a revolving restaurant. The view is a breathtaking panorama of the city. If you want to impress your other half, bring them here – *you're welcome*!

A gay night out in Berlin is an *experience* in its own right, especially Berghain. It's *so iconic* that "Berlin-style club" has become a well-worn phrase used by similar clubs from Tel Aviv to Bangkok to describe their vibe!

SCOTLAND

Landscapes full of wonder and gorgeous men who go commando under their kilts – Scotland *really* captured our hearts!

1 → FAVOURITE GAY CLUB
AXM, Glasgow

2 → FAVOURITE EVENT
Edinburgh Fringe Festival in August

3 → FAVOURITE LANDSCAPE
Duncansby Stacks, Caithness

4 → CULTURAL HIGHLIGHT
Trying peated whisky in Isle of Islay

5 → FAVOURITE ACTIVITY
Kayaking on Loch Ness

We'll never forget our road trip around the rugged Scottish countryside, where landscapes have inspired countless movies. We picked up our electric rental car in Edinburgh, and travelled across the entire country. Our electric car was easy to drive, and charging it became second nature thanks to Scotland's ChargePlace app, which helped us locate the nearest charging point – including free ones.

Scotland also has a large LGBTQ+ community, mainly concentrated in Glasgow and the capital, Edinburgh, each with its own lively gay scene. In just one day, Seby and I went from shaking our booties to Britney at Edinburgh's iconic CC Blooms to the peace and tranquillity of the Highlands.

Above all, we love the Scots. Laid-back, kind-hearted, and protective of one another, they don't tolerate seeing each other being picked on. As a gay couple we felt extremely comfortable travelling across the entire country. From booking a hotel room with a double bed to sitting down for a romantic meal, we were treated no differently than a straight couple would be.

LEFT Rocking our kilts at the Kinnoull Hill Woodland Park.

OUR TOP EXPERIENCES

✈ *Scotland*

1 → SASHAYING DOWN THE ROYAL MILE OF EDINBURGH

The Royal Mile is the quaint cobbled path in the Old Town of Edinburgh that bisects the city and links Edinburgh Castle and Holyrood Palace. For magnificent views over the city, there are two peaks we recommend visiting: Calton Hill and Arthur's Seat.

2 → THE GAY SCENE OF EDINBURGH

There was zero attitude, and the people were super friendly – they will come over and chat to you (especially after several rounds of drinks!). Around CC Blooms, there are a handful of other small gay bars to check out like Habana, Planet Bar & Kitchen, and The Street. Pride Edinburgh takes place in mid/late June.

3 → THE GAY SCENE OF GLASGOW

Whilst Edinburgh is the touristic hub of Scotland, Glasgow is the country's powerhouse. It also has the largest LGBTQ+ community in Scotland. The gay scene is based around the Merchant City area with bars like The Waterloo, Delmonicas, Underground, and clubs like AXM, The Polo Lounge, and Club X. Pride Glasgow takes place in mid/late June.

4 → EDINBURGH FRINGE FESTIVAL IN AUGUST

One of our favourite summer festivals. It is also one of the world's largest performance arts festivals, spanning 25 days. It includes drag shows, theatre, comedy, dance, circus, cabaret, musicals, opera, and music.

5 → KAYAKING ON LOCH NESS

Most will book a guided boat ride, but a more unique way to explore Loch Ness is by kayak (trying to spot Nessie, the mythical Loch Ness monster). Several companies around the loch offer guided kayaking tours.

6 → BEARSCOTFEST

BearScots is Scotland's group for bears, cubs, chubs, and their admirers. They organize monthly events in Edinburgh and Glasgow. In October they have a 4-day festival called BearScotFest that celebrates the best of the bears with dress up parties, events, and the presentation of the Bear of the Year title.

7 → STAY AT EAGLE BRAE NEAR GLEN AFFRIC

One of the most romantic and unique places we've stayed – a luxurious wooden cabin surrounded by the Highlands wilderness. It's also on the doorstep of the flourishing woodlands of Glen Affric National Nature Reserve. On one morning we awoke to see a couple of deers happily grazing just outside our cabin with no care in the world!

8 → DRIVE THROUGH LANDSCAPES SEEN IN THE JAMES BOND FILM *SKYFALL*

Those iconic scenes were filmed in Glencoe, and it became so famous that it is nicknamed Skyfall Road. This is the west side of the Scottish Highlands. The landscapes are irrefutably beautiful! The iconic Glenfinnan Viaduct is also nearby, and that carries the Hogwarts Express in the Harry Potter movies.

9 → DRINK WHISKY IN ISLAY

Islay is a charming wee island in the Hebrides in west Scotland that is famed for its peated whisky. It's 40km (25 miles) long, 24km (15 miles) wide, home to only 3,000 people, and yet this humble island packs in a whopping nine whisky distilleries! A whisky tour here is a must.

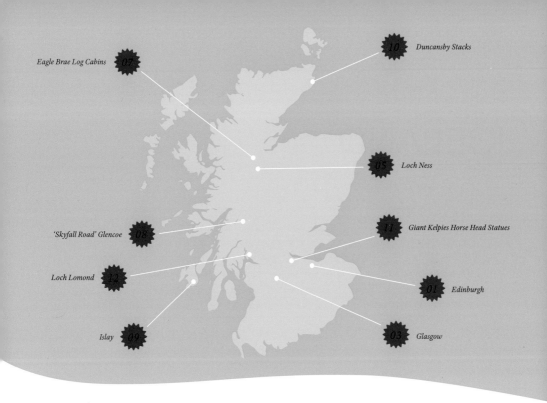

Duncansby Stacks — 10

Eagle Brae Log Cabins — 07

Loch Ness — 05

'Skyfall Road' Glencoe — 08

Giant Kelpies Horse Head Statues — 11

Loch Lomond — 12

Edinburgh — 01

Islay — 09

Glasgow — 03

10 → DUNCANSBY STACKS IN CAITHNESS

For us, THE best landscape in Scotland! It is two rugged pinnacles of rock dramatically jutting upwards from the sea's surface. It's a short walk to reach the stacks from the car park along the clifftops and easily worth it for the views. Best time to come is at sunset, but bring layers – the weather changes here fast!

11 → THE GIANT KELPIES HORSE HEAD STATUES

Where else in the world have you seen two colossal 30-metre-high horse head statues?! Kelpies are shape-shifting water creatures in Scottish folklore. These unique statues are located at the eastern entrance to the Forth and Clyde canal in Falkirk and are the largest equine sculptures in the world!

12 → HIKING IN LOCH LOMOND & THE TROSSACHS

Our favourite place in Scotland for hiking with a range of trails that pass steep mountain peaks, lakes, rolling hills, and forests. We did the trail up to the summit of Conic Hill. The views took our breath away (*literally, because it gets pretty windy up there*).

13 → CELEBRATE HOGMANAY

Hogmanay is the 3-day festival celebrating the Scottish New Year (late December, early January). Everyone in Scotland celebrates it, particularly the local LGBTQ+ community!

14 → CONNECT WITH THE COMMUNITY

If gay nightlife isn't your thing, we recommend checking out LGBT Health and Wellbeing. They run multiple events across the country for the Scottish LGBTQ+ community aimed at promoting a healthy lifestyle, from basketball to swimming. They also hold meet ups for specific sections of our community like Bi Nights or Trans Pride. There's also Kafe Kweer, a sober queer café-come-arts-space that serves vegan food, in Edinburgh.

ICELAND

1 → FAVOURITE GAY EVENT
Reykjavík Pride in August

2 → FAVOURITE EXPERIENCE
Seeing the Northern Lights

3 → FAVOURITE SOUVENIR
A *lopapeysa* (handmade Icelandic wool jumper)

4 → FAVOURITE MUSEUM
The Icelandic Phallological Museum, Reykjavík

5 → FAVOURITE LANDSCAPE
Skógafoss Waterfall

*I*celand is our all-time favourite road trip destination! We spent three unforgettable weeks traversing this enchanting country by car along the renowned Ring Road during the deep winter months, when a thick powdery snow enveloped everything in sight.

Along the way, we were treated to awe-inspiring sights of massive glaciers, erupting geysers, an abundance of geothermal baths, picturesque fjords, thrilling whale watching experiences, and encounters with the quirkiest and most delightful people – the charm of Icelandic humour is truly unmatched!

What left an indelible impression on us was Iceland's incredible gay-friendliness. Throughout our adventure, we felt completely at ease expressing our affection publicly, whether in the bustling capital city, Reykjavík, or in the most remote countryside settlement. Never once did anyone bat an eyelid at two men holding hands – acceptance and inclusivity were the norm.

It's no surprise, really. Iceland boasts some of the most progressive LGBTQ+ laws in the world, and it proudly made history with the appointment of the world's first openly gay head of state, Jóhanna Sigurðardóttir, in 2009.

Like most visitors, we departed Iceland with a profound sense of longing, already yearning to return for another enchanting chapter in this captivating land. Iceland has woven itself deeply into our hearts. Its allure is simply irresistible.

OUR TOP EXPERIENCES

1 → THE GAY SCENE OF REYKJAVÍK
With a population of just 130,000, the Icelandic capital has a few gay/queer-friendly bars such as Kíkí Queer Bar, Gaukurinn, and Bravó - along with two rainbow crossings celebrating the city's commitment to tolerance and diversity. Look out for Reykjavík Pride if heading there in August.

2 → CHECK OUT THE PENIS MUSEUM
You read that right! The Icelandic Phallological Museum in Reykjavík is the quirkiest place we've ever visited as well as the most fascinating – hosting an impressive collection of penises from over 300 specimens – as Shangela would say, *Halleloo*!

3 → RELAX IN THE BLUE LAGOON
A spa journey like no other, located in a lava field – the mineral-rich water and soft white silica mud have healing effects on the skin. . . *trust us, you'll feel like a goddess afterwards*!

4 → PAY HOMAGE TO EUROVISION
Húsavík is the home of Lars and Sigrit in the *brilliant* movie *Eurovision Song Contest: The Story of Fire Saga* that gave us *life* during the Covid lockdowns when Eurovision had to be cancelled! They have a bar/museum dedicated to it called Jaja Ding Dong. Húsavík is also the place to head for whale watching tours between May and September.

5 → BUY MATCHING *LOPAPEYSAS*
These are the handmade Icelandic wool jumpers worn by Icelanders to keep them warm in the deep winter months. We bought a matching pair from a shop in Húsavík. They're not cheap, but worth the expense as they really do keep you warm in the extreme cold. They also make for a terrific souvenir!

6 → SNORKEL BETWEEN TWO TECTONIC PLATES
Silfra Lake in the Thingvellir National Park is the only place in the world where you can snorkel between the Eurasian and North American tectonic plates. The water is so clear that when you're underwater, you can see up to 100m (328ft) away!

7 → WATCH A LIVE GEYSER ERUPT
The most dramatic one we saw was Strokkur in the Geysir Geothermal Area, which erupts every 5–10 minutes and can shoot water over 20m (66ft) high.

8 → GET SPLASHED BY A WORLD-FAMOUS WATERFALL
Iceland has an abundance of dramatic waterfalls. The most visited is Skógafoss which featured in *Game of Thrones, Thor: The Dark World*, and even in the music video for Justin Bieber's song *I'll Show You*.

9 → DIAMOND BEACH
Like no other beach we've ever been to – it has black volcanic sand decorated with large jewel-like chunks of ice, serving sparkling realness. The ice comes from the pieces of iceberg that break off from the nearby Breiðamerkurjökull glacier.

OUR PRACTICAL TIPS FOR LGBTQ+ TRAVELLERS

Iceland

1 → ROAD TRIP IN ICELAND

For independent travellers, we recommend renting a car with a company like Hertz Iceland to explore the country along its Ring Road. Quote PINK when booking and they can offer you a 10% discount. During the winter months, make sure it's a strong SUV/4WD vehicle as Icelandic roads can get pretty treacherous with the heavy snowfall. You'll also need to check the Icelandic Road and Coastal Administration website hourly for the latest info regarding road closures and driving conditions.

2 → GAY TRAVEL AGENTS

If you don't fancy a road trip you can easily base yourself in Reykjavík and arrange day trips via the excellent LGBTQ+ company, Pink Iceland. The best day trips we recommend are to Blue Lagoon, Sky Lagoon, and the Golden Circle. The Golden Circle tour will allow you to see Iceland's top three attractions: the Geysir Geothermal Area, Gullfoss Waterfall, and the Thingvellir National Park. Pink Iceland can also arrange tours to see the Northern Lights.

3 → HOW TO SEE THE NORTHERN LIGHTS

To maximize your chances of seeing the Northern Lights you need a dark, clear night sky. October to March is the optimal time for this. We recommend checking the Aurora Forecast website for the evening's aurora forecast or book yourself onto a tour from Reykjavík with a company like Pink Iceland.

4 → GAY-FRIENDLY HOTELS IN ICELAND

Any hotel is welcoming in Iceland – you'll have no problems here. The only issue you'll have is expense: Iceland is not cheap! Hotels we've tried, tested, and loved include the medium-priced Fosshotel chain, which has hotels all across the country including Reykjavík and Húsavík. For more budget-conscious travellers, we recommend Room With A View and Hotel Alda (both in Reykjavík).

5 → FOR THE ULTIMATE ROMANTIC SPLURGE

Book yourself into a suite at The Retreat at Blue Lagoon. It's one of the most luxurious hotels we've ever been to. Private lagoon from your balcony. . . *enough said!*

Left The Northern Lights. . .
STUNNING!

Giant glaciers, explosive geysers, a *multitude* of geothermal baths, *fabulous* fjords, whale watching, and the *quirkiest* people you'll ever meet – you can't beat Icelandic humour!

THE MIDNIGHT CALL!

↗ *Iceland*

To see the fabled Northern Lights, you have to be ready for the call!

We were tucked up in bed at the Fosshotel Glacier Lagoon in southeast Iceland, fast asleep.

Suddenly, the phone rang. It was *The Call!*

We'd asked the night receptionist to call and wake us if there had been any sightings of the Aurora Borealis, also known as the Northern Lights.

When you get *The Call*, EVERY second counts! You never know when the Aurora Borealis will disappear.

"Come on Stefan, get up. We need to get going!"

By the time Stefan opened his eyes, I was already fully dressed in my many layers of winter clothes (*Icelandic weather in the deep winter is rough!*), my camera to hand along with our tripod and a bag of snacks, ready to head.

Once Stefan was also ready, we rushed to our car. I'll never forget struggling to close the car door as I fought the powerful gust of wind! Our goal was to reach Diamond Beach, around a 20 minute drive away from our hotel. We had visited earlier that day and agreed we'd come to this spot to see the Northern Lights. As well as being completely isolated, it was far from any human settlement, therefore guaranteeing complete darkness at night.

The trick to seeing the Northern Lights is to head as close as you can to the Arctic Circle (Iceland sits just below it) where the Earth's magnetosphere interacts with the sun's rays to create the famed ethereal lights. In addition, the sky has to be completely dark with minimal light pollution and, of course, as clear as possible.

Every day, we checked the hourly weather forecast as well as the daily Aurora forecast on the *vedur.is* website that gives a mark out of 10 which determines the chances of seeing Northern Lights.

Both of us acted like two excited school children let loose in a candy shop!

Up until now, we hadn't been lucky, and our trip was almost over.

The adrenaline and anticipation we both felt during that drive was intense. We were acting like two excited school children let loose in a candy shop!

We eventually reached Diamond Beach, parked the car then scurried up the small hill using our phone torch to light the way through the freshly fallen thick snow.

When we reached the top, we looked up at the darkness. There was no one else around.

We waited patiently as the biting cold wind blew hard. I pulled in Stefan close to share our body heat. Despite the cold, I loved how cosy we felt!

Suddenly, a dash of green broke out in the darkness lighting up the night. Then another one. Then a third. . .

"Oh my God, Stefan, did you see that?!"

I was speechless. It was the Northern Lights!

As each ray of green light broke through the dark night we would point at them, smiling at each other, laughing with joy.

"Did you see that one? Over there, there's another one, look, Stefan!"

It was a celestial kaleidoscope of alien-like waves of greens dancing, like a giant lava lamp lighting up the sky. We were euphoric. Out there in the middle of the Icelandic countryside, pitch black and in the freezing cold, wrapped in the embrace of the love of my life, watching something so magnificent together: this is one of the most romantic moments of our lives that will live in our hearts and memories forever.

ITALY

"There's something magical in the air here, Stefan!" Seby says this to me every time we visit Italy – and admittedly, it's true!

**1 → FAVOURITE
GAY SCENE**
Porta Venezia, Milan

**2 → FAVOURITE
ROMANTIC
EXPERIENCE**
Venice

**3 → FAVOURITE
GAY EVENT**
Milano Pride

**4 → CULTURAL
HIGHLIGHT**
Exploring the ancient
parts of Rome

**5 → FAVOURITE
ROAD TRIP**
Puglia

*I*t all began in February 2010 when we visited Venice to celebrate our one-year anniversary. Despite the cold weather and the city's occasional floods, Venice cast an irresistible spell on us.

Since that magical trip, Italy's charm has beckoned us back year after year. Among our most cherished adventures was a mesmerizing road trip through Puglia. And Rome, oh, Rome! It left us utterly astounded as we marvelled at magnificent buildings with rich histories dating back hundreds, even thousands, of years.

Various places in Italy have inspired iconic films and TV series – such as Disney's *Luca* ("Silencio, Bruno!"), *The White Lotus* ("These gays, they're trying to murder me!"), and the infamous *Godfather* trilogy ("I'm going to make him an offer he can't refuse").

And who could forget chic Milan, Italy's fashion-capital? Eleganza extravaganza, indeed! When it comes to the gay scene, Milan leads the way. It has a pretty large gaybourhood in Porta Venezia. Every weekend, the crowds of each gay bar here converge on the pavements outside, creating a big gay street party!

Then there's the food. . . the beaches. . . the fashion. . . the arts. . . *and the men!*

RIGHT A romantic gondola ride in Venice.

OUR TOP EXPERIENCES
↗ *Italy*

1 → GET ROMANTIC IN VENICE

Our first trip together in Italy was in Venice. We loved everything about it: the wondrous canals, elegant palazzos, intricate bridges, gondola rides, and who could forget the iconic Piazza San Marco. What Venice lacks in a dedicated gay scene, it more than makes up for in romantic experiences.

2 → EXPLORING ROME

Every corner we turned we'd stumble on yet *another* historic marvel that brings the past to life and is so rich with history – the Trevi Fountain, the Colosseum, St. Peter's Basilica, the Sistine Chapel, the Pantheon, and Piazza Navona. Rome also has a small gay scene tucked away behind the Colosseum along the street called Via San Giovanni in the Laterano area, with bars like My Bar and Coming Out.

3 → FALLING IN LOVE IN FLORENCE

Like Venice, Florence is the place for romance and culture. It is home to Michelangelo's David, the Leonardo da Vinci Museum, and the Duomo Cathedral. Florence also has a small gay scene with gay bars like Queer and Piccolo Café and clubs like Crisco and Fabrik.

4 → ROAD TRIP THROUGH PUGLIA

Puglia is the southeastern region of Italy, with some of the best beaches in the country, including a few gay (clothing-optional) beaches like D'Ayala and Torre Guaceto. Make sure to stop at Lecce, Alberobello, Polignano a Mare, and Otranto – each with their unique architecture. The best gay hangouts to check out are the Pacha Mama club in Bari and Caffè Bellini in Gallipoli.

5 → MILAN, THE GAY CAPITAL OF ITALY

Whilst Milan has an impressive Cathedral (the Duomo di Milano), we love coming here for the gay scene of Porta Venezia. Other gay parties in Milan we love include La Boum, ONEWAY, Club Plastic, and BOTOX Matinèe.

6 → CELEB-SPOTTING ON THE AMALFI COAST

When we watched *Wonder Woman*, we were blown away by those stunning shots of the mythical island of Themyscira. It's actually the Amalfi Coast – 48km (30 miles) of stunning coastline along the southern edge of Italy's Sorrento Peninsula. It's so popular that celebrities are frequently spotted here from Rihanna and Beyoncé to Heidi Klum and Jennifer Lopez.

→ COUNTRY COUNTING!

As well as visiting Italy, country counting enthusiasts may be interested in adding two of the world's smallest countries to their lists: Vatican City in Rome and San Marino near Rimini. Vatican City is easy as it's located in central Rome. San Marino is a bit more tricky to reach: first you need to fly to Bologna and then take a one-hour train to Rimini, followed by a thirty-minute bus ride into San Marino.

05

7 → HIKING IN CINQUE TERRE

Translating to "Five Lands", Cinque Terre are five picturesque fishing villages in the Italian Riviera: Monterosso, Vernazza, Corniglia, Manarola, and Riomaggiore. You can hike between the towns – but first check which routes are open at the tourist office in Monterosso. We also recommend heading to the clothing-optional gay beach of Guvano.

8 → FOOD HEAVEN IN SICILY

Whether it's the Doric-style Greek temples, Byzantine mosaics, Roman theatres, or Mount Etna herself, Sicily is rich with beauty. For us, we loved Sicilian food – *arancini, pannelle, cannoli, sfincione, pani câ meusa...* we could go on forever!

ASIA

Inspired by Stefan's *obsession* with the Genghis Khan dynasty, we began our big Asia trip on the *Trans-Siberian train* from Moscow in Russia to Ulaanbaatar in Mongolia, stopping off along the way at places like Yekaterinburg and Irkutsk (for Lake Baikal). We then visited Mongolia, China, Nepal, India, the Maldives, Sri Lanka, Laos, Cambodia, Myanmar, Vietnam, Indonesia, the Philippines, and Taiwan.

Despite being a conservative continent, the people in Asia are respectful, humble, and they welcome foreigners. The *food is a joy* to discover – Japanese, Thai, Indian, and Sichuan are our personal favourites. Asia is also *rich in culture*, some dating back millennia, and not to mention *world wonders* like the Great Wall of China, the Taj Mahal, and Angkor Wat.

But, as we said, Asia is very conservative: in most Asian countries, LGBTQ+ rights are lagging. At the date of publication, *only one country* has legalized gay marriage: Taiwan. Other countries that are more tolerant (by Asian standards) and are well-known gay havens with *thriving gay scenes* include Thailand, Japan, Cambodia, Vietnam, and the Philippines.

↗ *Asia*

THAILAND

We always look for an excuse to return every year. It's our happy place in the world, and the place we both love in equal measure.

1 → FAVOURITE CLUB
DJ Station, Bangkok

2 → FAVOURITE BAR FOR DRAG SHOWS
The Stranger, Bangkok

3 → FAVOURITE GAY EVENT
White Party Bangkok in December

4 → FAVOURITE ISLAND
Koh Lipe

5 → FAVOURITE FOOD
Som tum
(spicy papaya salad)

1 0s! 10s! 10s! across the board...
Dolled up in our finest tight short shorts and skimpy tank tops, Seby always insists on sashaying into the narrow side street of Silom Soi 4. I don't quite know what it is about Bangkok but whenever my shy, demure Frenchman's in town, something switches inside of him. It's as if a roaring sassy, dragon comes alive and he becomes the life and soul of the party!

Beyond Bangkok, Thailand has some of the best beaches we've ever been to, along with thriving coral reefs, making it a paradise for scuba divers.

And then there's the food, a delectable affair that never fails to tantalize. From the classic pad thai to the sticky mango rice and the flavoursome *som tum*, along with mouth-watering curries – every meal is a culinary adventure!

As gay travellers, Thailand welcomes us with open arms. The warm-hearted, humble, and accepting nature of the Thai people is evident in every encounter. Buddhism, the dominant religion, embraces tolerance and acceptance, creating an atmosphere of genuine inclusivity. In this country, we feel free to be ourselves, and our love as a gay couple is met with complete respect.

At worst, they ask if we're brothers!

LEFT Nomadic Boys to Hammock Boys... chilling on Koh Lipe's Sunrise Beach.

OUR TOP EXPERIENCES
✈ *Thailand*

1 → THE GAY SCENE OF BANGKOK
Silom Soi 4 is where you'll start your night, but never where you'll finish. . . This crazy, bustling street is the pulsating heart of Bangkok's gay scene. Bars like Circus, The Balcony, and The Stranger adorn the pavements inviting you to join in the excitement every evening. A few blocks away is Silom Soi 2 where the crowds head to after 11p.m. to party at gay clubs like DJ Station.

2 → CULTURAL HUB OF CHIANG MAI
We immersed ourselves in a world of ancient rituals and rich traditions at Chiang Mai. With over 300 Buddhist temples in and around the old city, this was our first foray into Buddhism. Amidst its charm, we also discovered a small but vibrant gay scene with hangouts like Adam's Apple Club and Ram Bar.

3 → LOOK AFTER AN ELEPHANT
We recommend visiting the Elephant Rescue Park in Chiang Mai. The sanctuary offers a haven for elephants rescued from unethical riding companies and circuses (please do not ride the elephants and support this industry – the elephants are beaten into submission). Up close, we discovered the unique personalities of these gentle giants by feeding, bathing, brushing, and hugging them – this is an experience you'll never forget!

4 → MAYA BAY COVE ON KOH PHI PHI
A paradise come to life! Koh Phi Phi attracts countless visitors thanks to the famous movie *The Beach*. The beach in question is none other than Maya Bay Cove!

5 → VISIT KRABI PROVINCE
Railay beach and the dramatic limestone karsts are reason alone to head to Krabi. The Tiger Cave temple (Wat Tham Sua) is another highlight. It's part of a temple complex containing a maze of natural caves where monks live, all surrounded by lush jungle.

6 → GET PADI CERTIFIED IN KOH TAO
This is the place we learnt to scuba dive and we've been hooked ever since! Koh Tao has a large scuba diving community thanks to its abundance of affordable diving schools. The pristine waters around the island make it the perfect spot for beginner divers.

→ KOH TARUTAO – THE ULTIMATE ROBINSON CRUSOE EXPERIENCE!

This large uninhabited island close to Koh Lipe is protected by the government. There are no commercial businesses here, only the camping grounds and a few restaurants run by the national park. There's so much to do: snorkelling, beaches, biking, jungle treks, and our favourite – kayaking through the mangrove forest to a crocodile cave. The crocs are long gone, but the experience is just as thrilling!

06

7 → CELEBRATE PRIDE IN KOH SAMUI

Located next to party island Koh Pha Ngan, Koh Samui is the more chilled sister island, also popular with gay travellers. The Alpha gay resort is a gay institution on the island, spearheading Koh Samui Pride in April. The island also has a gay bar to check out called Pride Bar.

8 → KOH LIPE

Our favourite island in Thailand – you'll find us here every January! It's quite remote and difficult to reach, but it's not as busy as other Thai islands. The water is crystal clear, especially at Sunrise Beach. Step into the water and you'll see Nemo (clown fish) and all his friends everywhere!

9 → GAY PARTIES IN THAILAND

There are a number of circuit parties happening in Thailand throughout the year. The most famous are the Songkran G Circuit in Bangkok in April, Circuit Festival in Pattaya in June, and the White Party in Bangkok in December. These are renowned for being some of the best gay events in Asia.

10 → DELICIOUS STREET FOOD

Eating out in the streets of Thailand is one of the most rewarding and authentic culinary experiences you can have. Our advice is, if it's full of locals, you know you're in for a treat!

INDIA

India is a cultural blast! It's a treat for the senses; with aromatic smells, vibrant colours, and the hustle and bustle of people.

1 → FAVOURITE LANDMARK
Taj Mahal

2 → CULTURAL HIGHLIGHT
The Ghats of Varanasi

3 → FAVOURITE FOOD
Kerala fish molee curry

4 → FAVOURITE ROMANTIC MEMORY
Sailing on a houseboat on the Kerala backwaters

5 → MOST BIZARRE MEMORY
Erotic sculptures of Khajuraho

*A*midst this mesmerizing chaos, we found ourselves marvelling at stunning temples, grand castles, and even cows confidently stopping traffic!

Even after spending a month traversing this vast land, we felt like we had only scratched the surface. The country is so immense that it feels like a mini continent in itself.

Our journey began in northern India, leading us through New Delhi to the iconic Taj Mahal, a testament to eternal love, in nearby Agra. Our first steps through the bustling streets of New Delhi were a revelation. The first thing we noticed were men walking the streets holding hands. No, it wasn't Pride, but a tradition deep-rooted in south Asia whereby men are *very* tactile around each other. It's not about sexual attraction, simply an everyday cultural norm... *one that confused the hell out of our gaydar!*

We ventured into the enchanting region of Rajasthan and embarked on unforgettable train rides that were experiences of their own. The unique temples of Khajuraho and the spiritual magnetism of Varanasi added depth to our adventure. We also explored the tranquil charm of Kerala in southern India, a soothing contrast to the busy, metropolitan north.

RIGHT The Taj Mahal. *Just wow!*

OUR TOP EXPERIENCES

India

1 → EMBRACE YOUR INNER PRINCESS DI AT THE TAJ MAHAL

Already a famous Wonder of the World, the Taj Mahal became even more prominent when the late Princess Diana posed here in 1992. The Taj Mahal is magnificent: the heaving crowds, *less magnificent!* For this reason, we strongly advise coming at sunrise.

2 → THE PINK CITY IN RAJASTHAN

Jaipur is so nicknamed after the buildings were painted a terracotta pink in 1876 by the Maharaja Raj Singh to welcome Queen Victoria's husband, Prince Albert. Jaipur also has some of the most impressive palaces and temples we've seen.

3 → THE GAY SCENE IN NEW DELHI

During the day we explored attractions like The Red Fort, but at night we checked out the small underground gay scene. Thankfully, since our visit, more gay parties and venues have thrived in Delhi including Kitty Su at The LaLiT.

4 → VISIT "THE CITY OF THE DEAD"

Varanasi is unlike anything we've ever seen before. It's the holiest place for Hindus who head here to bathe in the sacred Ganges River or to cremate their dead along the ghats (riverfront steps) – where the city's nickname comes from. With all this activity going on daily, imagine how unique a walk along the sacred riverbank is! It's even more dazzling during a festival like Diwali, the festival of lights.

5 → THE GAY SCENE IN MUMBAI

As the fashion capital of India, Mumbai is a joy for shopping. It's also the gay party capital of India! The main queer venues still thriving include The Ghetto and Cafe Mondegar. We also recommend checking out the ad hoc gay parties organized by Salvation Star.

6 → DIVERSITY AND TOLERANCE IN GOA

For years, Goa has been a hippie haven welcoming one and all, making it a popular LGBTQ+ destination. Yoga retreats and wellness resorts are all the rage in Goa, but the region is also famed for its laid-back beaches, plantation tours, and natural parks.

08

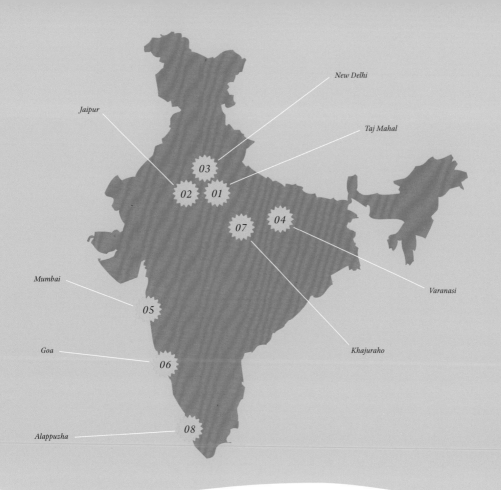

New Delhi

Jaipur

Taj Mahal

03

02 *01*

04

07

Mumbai

Varanasi

05

Goa

Khajuraho

06

08

Alappuzha

7 → THE EROTIC SCULPTURES OF KHAJURAHO

Whilst the Hindu and Jain temples in Khajuraho are truly remarkable to behold, they often make the headlines in travel guides because of the more *explicit* sculptures! The Khajuraho Temples are famous for celebrating the erotic arts and depict various erotic positions representing sexual liberation through the sculptures!

8 → CRUISING ALONG THE BACKWATERS OF KERALA

A scenic network of lagoons, canals, and lakes lined with coconut trees, paddy fields, and beaches. Renting a houseboat from Alappuzha is the best way to take it all in over a few days. This was our most romantic experience in India – pure bliss drifting peacefully through this captivating landscape together.

9 → RIDE ON AN INDIAN TRAIN

Whether you're visiting the Taj Mahal in Agra from Delhi or heading to Varanasi on an overnight train from Jaipur, a ride on an Indian train is *an experience!* They are notoriously late – once we waited 5 hours for one train! But once inside, it's full of life and character.

Our tip: if travelling independently, book your train on the IRCTC website as far in advance as you can – remember this is a country with a population of over 1.4 billion so you can imagine demand can be pretty high!

Whilst the Hindu and Jain temples in Khajuraho are truly *remarkable* to behold, they often make the headlines in travel guides because of the more *explicit* sculptures!

OUR PRACTICAL TIPS FOR LGBTQ+ TRAVELLERS

✈ India

1 → INDIA IS CONSERVATIVE

Whilst attitudes are changing, the LGBTQ+ community still faces challenges in society. As a foreigner you get away with a lot more than local gay guys. However, we advise erring on the side of caution when it comes to public displays of affection.

2 → BOOKING A DOUBLE BED

Booking a double bed in any of the places we stayed at in India was never a problem. All the staff we dealt with were respectful and never once made us feel like second-class citizens. This speaks volumes for how much Indians really value foreigners – both straight and gay.

3 → GAY TOUR OR INDEPENDENT TRAVEL

We did our trip independently, but there are a handful of excellent gay tour companies that run trips in India throughout the year. These include Out Adventures, HE Travel, CODA Tours, and Brand g Vacations.

4 → OVERNIGHT GUESTS

A lot of hotel staff don't take too kindly to overnight guests, particularly local gay guys staying over. If you want to host overnight guests, consider booking an Airbnb or misterb&b instead of a hotel room.

5 → EAT EVERYTHING. . . BUT BE CAUTIOUS!

Food is reason alone to go to India! Dining out is always a treat: inexpensive, and a joy for the palate. A couple of tips to avoid an upset stomach; avoid drinking tap water, ask for no spices if you're sensitive to spicy food, avoid peeled fruit (peel them yourself), and stick to vegetables that have been well cooked. We also recommend steering clear of salads and any foods potentially washed with tap water.

→ GAY BOLLYWOOD!

We're LIVING for Bollywood movies that explore LGBTQ+ relationships in a positive light. A few to check out include: Badhaai Do (2022), Bomgay (1996), I Am (2010), My Brother. . . Nikhil (2005), and Aligarh (2016).

Seby

"WHEN THE MUSIC STOPS..."

India

Before 2018, LGBTQ+ folk in India faced an anti-gay law.

*I*ndia was the first country I had ever visited with an anti-gay law, so I was nervous before coming here. Our first visit to India in 2014 was just after the reintroduction of Section 377 of the 1861 Indian Penal Code by the Indian Supreme Court, which criminalized gay sex and carries a punishment of up to ten years in prison. So, imagine my angst at the time!

Given New Delhi's size (35 million), we were expecting it to have some sort of active gay scene. Unfortunately, most online resources about gay hangouts in Delhi were outdated at the time: all openly gay hangouts had either shut down or been forced underground.

Using Grindr, we were able to tap into the local underground gay scene to discover the venue of that week's party: Knight by Castle 9 at Connaught Place.

So, dolled up and ready to roll, we hit the town!

The party was a lot of fun: it was heaving with locals, dancing to Kylie, drinking, flirting – just having a gay old time! Just as we whipped out our phones to grab a few selfies, a burly bouncer quickly took us aside and sternly told us that all photography is strictly prohibited. Their job is to protect the clientele who were sensitive about their families and employers finding out they'd been to a gay club.

We continued to dance – Lady Gaga's *Alejandro* was pumping away on the speakers.

Suddenly, at around 1a.m., the music stopped!

All the lights were switched off and window blinds hastily pulled down. Everybody was asked to stay inside the club, be silent and, under no circumstances, go outside.

The police had arrived!

Everyone in the club was blasé about it. Apparently, this happens all the time, every week!

However, I was freaking out...

What are your rights if arrested in India? What's the number of the French embassy?

How the hell am I going to explain this to my poor mother who was already worried sick about our trip?!

Our gay Indian friends in the club reassured us, explaining that the policemen were simply looking for a cash bribe from the party promoter and would leave everyone else alone.

inside to avoid antagonizing the police and in around ten minutes we would be allowed to leave.

The bouncer was right! The policemen's bribes were swiftly settled, and everyone was allowed to leave the club via the back door, one by one. No one got hurt and no one was arrested.

Since the legalization of homosexuality in 2018, things have massively improved for the Indian LGBTQ+ community. Gay

---

The party was a lot of fun: it was heaving with locals, dancing to Kylie, drinking, flirting – just having a gay old time.

It was just the way it had always been!

We waited for around twenty minutes. At one point one young guy tried to leave through the back door, but the burly bouncer grabbed him and held him tight. In a firm but calm tone he told us that everything is okay, but we had to wait

parties are allowed to operate openly and harassment from local police for being gay is a thing of the past. The Indian LGBTQ+ community stands stronger and more confident than ever, fearlessly lobbying the government for additional laws to safeguard LGBTQ+ people.

Asia

VIETNAM

We fell in love with Vietnam! As avid foodies, we delighted in exploring the Vietnamese cuisine.

1 → FAVOURITE GAY BAR
ChinChin Bar,
Hồ Chí Minh

2 → FAVOURITE LANDSCAPE
Hạ Long Bay

3 → FAVOURITE FOOD
Cao lầu
(pork noodle dish)

4 → FAVOURITE DRINK
Cà phê trứng
(egg coffee)

5 → CRAZIEST MEMORY
Trying to cross the streets of Hồ Chí Minh!

"Forget about it Stefan. I'm NOT crossing that!" Seby refused to move!

Panic set in as we stood at the side of the road for what seemed like an eternity, gazing at the chaotic jungle of traffic unfolding before our eyes: a mesmerizing dance of mopeds swirling from all directions, miraculously weaving through one another without a single collision!

"Come on guys, just take my hand and follow my lead!" said our Vietnamese friend Quan who was trying to show us how to navigate the crazy traffic of the streets of Hồ Chí Minh (also referred to locally as Saigon).

"Just walk through it slowly and carefully. Never stop, never go back, and the traffic will just go around you!" Quan said to us. He wasn't wrong!

Beyond the mayhem of traffic, it has a rich cultural heritage with influences from China and, more recently, from when it was a French colony (1877–1954). This is reflected in the cuisine; for example, the ever-popular Vietnamese staple, baguette sandwiches (bánh mì).

We spent a month travelling in this unique S-shaped nation, from the bustling streets of Hồ Chí Minh in the south to the vibrant capital of Hanoi in the north, passing through the enchanting cities of Huế and Da Nang in the central region. Each new destination presented us with a delectable revelation, which we share on the next few pages!

LEFT Our romantic cruise in Hạ Long Bay.

OUR TOP EXPERIENCES

✈ *Vietnam*

1 → GAY NIGHT OUT IN HỒ CHÍ MINH
This city has the largest LGBTQ+ community in Vietnam with a mix of locals and expats. Because of this, the gay scene is quite extensive, with gay hangouts like Thi Bar, ChinChin Bar, Frolic, and Les Come Out.

Our foodie highlight in Hồ Chí Minh
Bánh mì (baguette sandwiches).

2 → CỦ CHI TUNNELS
An extensive network of underground tunnels built by the Viet Cong soldiers during the Vietnam War (1954–1975) as a place to hide themselves and their supplies from the American soldiers. Củ Chi is a rural district of Hồ Chí Minh, located around 40km (25 miles) northwest of the city centre and easy to reach by taxi or local public bus.

Our foodie highlight in Củ Chi
Cơm tấm (broken rice usually eaten with pork).

3 → CRUISE THE MEKONG DELTA
A vast maze of rivers, swamps, and islands, located to the west of Hồ Chí Minh. It has floating markets, Khmer pagodas, and villages surrounded by rice paddies. It's nicknamed "the rice bowl of Vietnam" because most of the country's fresh produce is produced here.

Our foodie highlight in the Mekong Delta
Bún mắm (fermented thick vermicelli soup).

4 → VISIT THE IMPERIAL CITY OF HUẾ
The former capital city of Vietnam (1802–1945) and the heart of the Nguyen dynasty, the last royal dynasty of Vietnam. Today, the Imperial City within Huế is a UNESCO World Heritage Site containing the former imperial family's palaces, shrines, intricate pagodas, tombs, and impressive gardens.

Our foodie highlight in Huế
Bún bò Huế (spicy soup with beef).

5 → GO BACK IN TIME IN HỘI AN'S OLD TOWN
Once a bustling Asian trading port town, the old town is now a UNESCO World Heritage Site. We loved getting lost in the maze of narrow cobblestone streets, particularly in the evening when they were lit up by colourful paper lanterns. Stefan teased me saying it was so romantic that he could imagine many wedding proposals being made here!

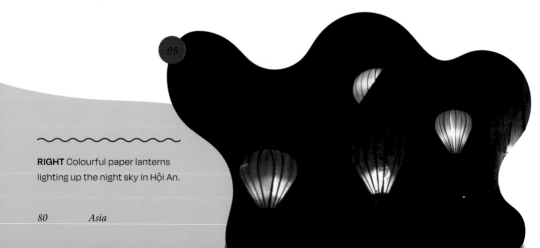

05

RIGHT Colourful paper lanterns lighting up the night sky in Hội An.

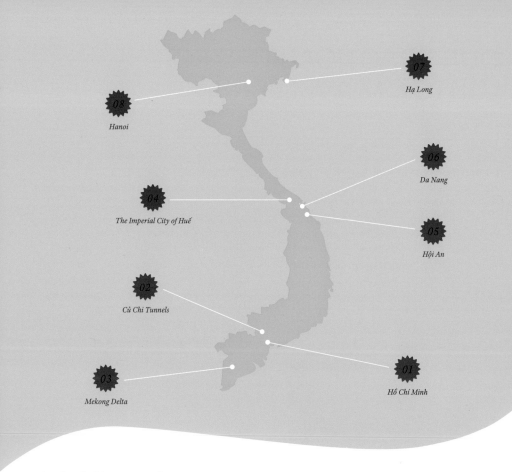

07
Hạ Long

08
Hanoi

06
Da Nang

04
The Imperial City of Huế

05
Hội An

02
Củ Chi Tunnels

03
Mekong Delta

01
Hồ Chí Minh

Our foodie highlight in Hội An
Cao lầu (pork and vegetable noodles, and also Stefan's favourite).

6 → THE GOLDEN BRIDGE OF DA NANG
A 150-metre-long (492ft) pedestrian golden bridge with two giant hand sculptures in the middle that gives the impression that it's being held up by the Hands of God! The bridge is located at the Sun World Ba Na Hills amusement park near Da Nang.

Our foodie highlight in Da Nang
Mì Quảng (noodles with meat and herbs, and also Seby's favourite).

7 → HẠ LONG BAY CRUISE
An absolute must-see! This UNESCO World Heritage Site boasts 1,600 islands, each sculpted into ancient limestone pillars that were formed thousands of years ago. We went on a romantic three-day cruise, which included unforgettable moments of kayaking and snorkelling amid the turquoise waters.

Our foodie highlight in Hạ Long
Bánh cuốn (steamed rice rolls usually stuffed with pork and mushrooms).

8 → WATER PUPPET SHOW IN HANOI
The art of water puppetry originated in the 11th century in the Red River Delta, north Vietnam. Today, you can see this ancient art at Hanoi's Thăng Long Water Puppet Theatre.

Our foodie highlights in Hanoi
Phở (noodle soup and the National Dish of Vietnam) and cà phê trứng (egg coffee).

OUR PRACTICAL TIPS FOR LGBTQ+ TRAVELLERS

✈ *Vietnam*

1 → VIETNAM IS SAFE FOR GAY TRAVELLERS

We found Vietnam to be one of the most gay-friendly countries in Asia. We never had any problems getting a double bed in any of the hotels or guesthouses we stayed at and all hotel staff we encountered had no issue about welcoming a gay couple. At no stage did we ever encounter any homophobia, but we did get asked *"Are you twins because you look the same"* a lot!

2 → VIETNAM IS PROGRESSIVE

Even though society is conservative we found the Vietnamese to be tolerant. This is not surprising given they've never had any anti-gay laws and also have progressive laws for people living with HIV/AIDS, which includes anti-discrimination and free health care. They also banned conversion therapy in 2022, and in the same year declassified homosexuality and transgender identity as an illness.

3 → GAY TOURS IN VIETNAM

There are several tour companies offering gay tours in Vietnam including HE Travel and Brand g Vacations.

→ NOTABLE LGBTQ+ VIETNAMESE MOVIES TO CHECK OUT

- *Lost in Paradise (2011)*
- *Madam Phung's Last Journey (2014)*
- *Finding Phong (2015)*
- *Goodbye Mother (2019)*
- *Bridge of Destiny (2020)*

ABOVE Golden Bridge, Da Nang.

We spent a month travelling in this *unique* S-shaped nation, from the *bustling* streets of Hồ Chí Minh in the south to the *vibrant* capital of Hanoi in the north, passing through the *enchanting* cities of Huế and Da Nang in the central region.

Asia

JAPAN

It's easy to fall in love with Japan. Trust us, we've been back on three separate trips and we're keen to return for more!

1 → FAVOURITE GAY SCENE
Ni-chōme area of Shinjuku, Tokyo

2 → FAVOURITE GAY EVENT
Hakuba Rainbow Festival in March

3 → FAVOURITE ONSEN
Mannenyu in Shinjuku, Tokyo

4 → CULTURAL HIGHLIGHT
Dressing up like geishas!

5 → FAVOURITE ACTIVITY
Scuba diving in the Yaeyama Islands

Welcome to the future! That's how we felt in Japan. Everything feels so advanced and works meticulously. From the impressive Shinkansen bullet trains, robot-run capsule hotels, high-tech toilets, to the maze of vending machines on every other street corner that sell anything you can possibly need like alcohol, ice cream, eggs, tights, umbrellas. . . even condoms!

The Japanese do everything with unparalleled precision and immaculate attention to detail – and always with a smile that radiates genuine hospitality. Every little facet of day-to-day life is based on a tradition that dates back thousands of years, which manifests in the way people behave towards each other.

For example, instead of the customary handshake to greet someone, they instead gracefully bow to each other – a practice from the Yayoi period. The depth of the bow conveys the level of formality and respect one wishes to extend to the other person.

As a gay couple exploring the wonders of Japan, we found ourselves welcomed with open arms. Throughout our journey, we encountered no hint of homophobia, seamlessly checking into hotels and securing a double bed without any hesitation. The inclusive atmosphere enveloped us, and we never once faced judgmental glances. Instead, we were met with genuine respect from everyone we encountered.

~~~~~~

LEFT Tsūtenkaku Tower soaring over downtown Osaka.

OUR TOP EXPERIENCES

✈ *Japan*

1 → THE GAY SCENE OF TOKYO
The Ni-chōme area of Shinjuku has the world's highest concentration of gay bars: over 300 crammed together into a row! The ones we loved and recommend are Arty Farty, Campy! Bar, AiiRO, and New Sazae. We also suggest looking out for the VITA gay parties that take place in Tokyo throughout the year.

2 → BEAT THE JET LAG IN AN ONSEN
We found this to be the perfect way to relax, especially after a long-haul flight. An onsen is a public bath with various pools of water sourced from hot springs, each heated to a different temperature. Bathing must be naked and therefore men and women are separated into two separate sections. It feels liberating bathing stark naked with other men!

3 → GAY SKI WEEK DURING HAKUBA RAINBOW FESTIVAL
Takes place over two weekends every March in one of the ski resorts in the Hakuba Valley. As well as glorious skiing, the festival also includes a range of lively après-ski events with drag shows, trivia nights, pub crawls, and themed parties.

4 → THE GAY SCENE OF OSAKA
This is the second largest gay scene in Japan. Like Tokyo, Osaka has a large concentration of over 100 gay bars based in the Dōyamachō district. Our favourites were Grand Slam (for karaoke), Dungaree (which has more of a bear vibe), as well as Bull and FrenZy-FrenZy. EXPLOSION is the best gay club in Osaka, in our humble opinion.

5 → KYOTO TEMPLES AND SHRINES
Kyoto is the cultural heart of Japan, *packed* with the most impressive shrines, sites, and temples we've ever seen. Our favourites include the Kinkaku-ji, the Fushimi Inari Shrine, and the Sagano Bamboo Forest in the Arashiyama district. Kyoto also has a small gay scene with hangouts like AZURE, Apple, and WORLD KYOTO.

6 → HIROSHIMA PEACE MEMORIAL MUSEUM
We think everyone needs to visit to learn about the tragedy inflicted on Hiroshima and Nagasaki at the end of World War Two. The museum stresses to never again resort to the brutal act of using nuclear weapons. Like Kyoto, Hiroshima has a small gay scene with bars like Goli Macho and Nagomi.

7 → VISIT THE ITSUKUSHIMA SHRINE
Located around one hour away from Hiroshima on an island, this unique and beautiful shrine stands upright in the water. It is particularly striking at sunset.

07

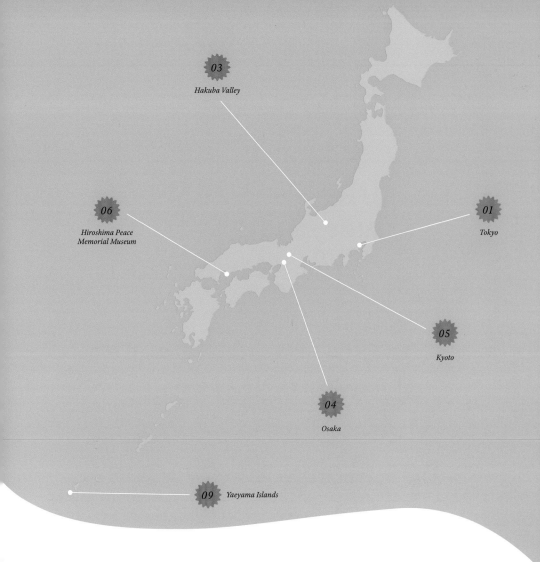

03 Hakuba Valley

06 Hiroshima Peace Memorial Museum

01 Tokyo

05 Kyoto

04 Osaka

09 Yaeyama Islands

8 → GO ON A GASTRONOMIC ADVENTURE
Take our advice and try everything! Highlights include fresh sushi from one of the many restaurants by the Toyosu Fish Market in Tokyo (one of the largest fish markets in the world), *okonomiyaki* (often called "Japanese pizza" – the best are in Hiroshima and Osaka), *ramen*, *wagyu* beef, *gyoza*, and *tempura* – all washed down with *sake*!

9 → TROPICAL GETAWAY IN THE YAEYAMA ISLANDS
These are Japan's southernmost inhabited islands. The islands have long stretches of white sandy beaches and are surrounded by pristine coral reefs. Our highlight was scuba diving with manta rays near Ishigaki island.

10 → ADMIRE THE ICONIC CHERRY BLOSSOMS
To really make your Insta pics pop, consider visiting either in spring (March–April) or autumn (October–November). Spring is the sakura (cherry blossom season) when the cherry trees bloom.

The Japanese do everything with *unparalleled* precision and *immaculate* attention to detail – and always with a smile that radiates *genuine* hospitality. Every little facet of day-to-day life is based on a tradition that dates back *thousands of years*.

OUR PRACTICAL TIPS FOR LGBTQ+ TRAVELLERS

Japan

1 → YOU'LL BE JUST FINE

Whilst the LGBTQ+ laws of Japan are slowly catching up with its more tolerant neighbour, Taiwan, we've never experienced any form of homophobia anywhere in Japan. The Japanese are one of the most respectful peoples we've ever met. There was never any issue booking a hotel. It's also a very safe country with an astonishingly low crime rate despite being one of the most densely populated nations.

2 → AVOID TOUCHING PEOPLE YOU MEET

The Japanese are shy about touching people they've just met. A common greeting is to put your hands in a prayer position and bow to each other instead of a handshake.

3 → AVOID TIPPING

In Japan, tips are regarded as an insult. The final price includes tipping and service – so just leave it at that to avoid accidental offence.

4 → COVER YOUR TATTOOS

Tattoos are stigmatized in Japan because they are associated with gangs. If going to a public gym, try to cover them up. If you want to go to an onsen (hot spring), you'll need to check if they are "tattoo-friendly" beforehand. Mannenyu in Shinjuku is one of the best tattoo-friendly onsens we've been to.

→ GAY-FRIENDLY TRAVEL GUIDES

For anything gay in Japan, whether a tour or general advice, we cannot recommend highly enough the services of the Tokyo-based gay company Out Asia. They offer a range of gay tours all over the country led by local LGBTQ+ guides. . . and sometimes even a few drag queens!

"FROM NOMADIC BOYS TO NOMADIC GEISHA"

✈ *Japan*

This was one transformation we will never forget!

"*As Sayuri was standing beneath the cherry tree, speaking to the one man she loved but could not have, a sprinkle of delicate pale pink petals fell upon them like snow. . .*"

At this point, Stefan grabbed the remote control, interrupting the most beautiful moment of *Memoirs of a Geisha* to declare:

"*SEBY – I know what your next birthday present is going to be!*"

A trip to the theatre? A musical, maybe? A Japanese-themed romantic dining experience with sake?

No, not quite. Nothing with my Stefan is ever obvious or predictable.

A few weeks later, I find myself in Morishita, a suburb of Tokyo, trying to locate the Studio Geisha Café. Turns out he'd booked us in for a complete geisha transformation for my birthday present!

I was really excited. I've always been fascinated by geisha culture – its origins, the elaborate make up, all the prep. . . I've been talking about it to Stefan for years, making him sit through countless viewings of *Memoirs of a Geisha*.

On that note, a quick word about cultural appropriation: this is not in any way intended to mock or poke fun at Japanese geisha culture. Our intention was simply to discover more about it and celebrate this fascinating and wonderful cultural facet of Japan!

Arriving at the Studio Geisha Café, we were greeted by Michiru, who showed us around. Michiru is a former model and actress. She set up the Studio Geisha Café with her husband to give people the chance to feel like they're in the skin of a real geisha and live out their dream. Interestingly, half of their customers are Japanese straight men!

We were fortunate to be her first foreign male geisha.

After introductions were over, Michiru sat us down, explained the process (she warned us it would take around three hours!) and then we started.

First, we had to select a beautiful traditional kimono. Stefan, who always insists on making a statement, chose

one that was bright pink and purple. I opted for a more chic, classical black kimono.

Next, we undressed and put on the *hada-juban* undergarment along with the distinct *tabi* socks. The socks divide your toes into two: one space for the big toe and the other for the remaining toes. This allows you to walk gracefully whilst wearing the tall wooden *okobo* shoes.

The most distinguishing feature of geisha is their elaborate *shironuri* makeup. I was always curious about its origin: Michiru explained that *shironuri*

After the makeup was completed, we were ready for our wigs. Geisha wigs are based on the *shimada* hairstyle of gathering the hair at the crown of the head and having a portion of the bun sectioned off to point outward.

Finally, our kimonos were fitted and our pouts perfected, we carefully hobbled over to the full-length mirror – *those okobo wooden shoes aren't the easiest to walk in!*

"*Gorgeous! Gorgeous!*" cried out Michiru.

Words cannot describe how I felt.

We were fortunate to be her first foreign male geisha.

was traditionally applied to showcase a young, beautiful face in dark candlelit rooms before electricity was invented. In our case, several layers of foundation had to be applied to hide our beard shadows (despite arriving freshly shaven!).

After that, our thick bushy eyebrows had to be hidden. To achieve this, a special wax was applied to cover them so that Michiru could then paint new thin eyebrows just above them.

Seeing our faces painted in *shironuri* makeup was already quite startling. But the most transformative moment was watching how dramatically our faces changed as our eyebrows were hidden and new ones painted on.

The person staring back at me in that mirror was *unrecognizable!* I could see the arms, head, shoulders moving as I commanded, but the elaborate white-faced being that was staring back at me bore no resemblance to the masculine reflection I was so used to seeing in my day-to-day life.

It was astonishing, and I'll be honest, it was also a little unnerving just how much my appearance was altered – to the point where I had to double take to realize that this dazzling geisha in the mirror was, in fact, me!

Bravo, my Stefan – a birthday present I won't forget in a hurry!

THE PHILIPPINES

Almost every backpacker we met in Southeast Asia told us the same thing – they came to the Philippines and ended up leaving completely besotted with the place!

1 → FAVOURITE HOTEL
Flower Island Resort, Big Budacan Island

2 → FAVOURITE ISLAND
Coron Island

3 → FAVOURITE DIVING SPOT
El Nido, Palawan Island

4 → FAVOURITE BEACH
Puka Shell Beach, Boracay Island

5 → FAVOURITE CLUB
O Bar, Manila

We can totally see why. With 7,641 islands that straddle the Coral Triangle, it is a paradise for underwater adventurers and tropical beach lovers. There is also an exciting and unique cuisine to discover that is influenced by former colonizers: the USA and Spain. The best thing about the Philippines, though, is the people. The Filipinos are well-known for their hospitality – *Filipino hospitality* is an actual *thing* here!

And most importantly, the Philippines is pretty gay-friendly – one of the most welcoming places for LGBTQ+ travellers in Asia. Obviously, we need to add an important caveat here. The Philippines is in no way on par with countries in West Europe and the Americas when it comes to LGBTQ+ rights, but when compared to other nations in Asia, it's up there with Thailand, Taiwan, and Japan, in our experience.

LEFT Seby and the palm tree at Flower Island Resort on Big Budacan Island.

OUR TOP EXPERIENCES
✈ *The Philippines*

1 → DIVING AND SNORKELLING IN EL NIDO

We did some of our best dives around El Nido on Palawan Island. The waters here are rich with tropical fish, turtles, and reef sharks. Whilst you can book yourself on a scuba diving trip, a cheaper way to enjoy the sea life here is on one of the many snorkelling trips.

2 → TROPICAL BEACH FUN IN BORACAY

Boracay has become one of the major LGBTQ+ destinations in the Philippines thanks to its white sandy beaches, nightlife, and world-class gay-friendly hotels like Mandala Spa & Resort Villas. White Beach is often singled out as *the* place to head, but we recommend heading to the northern tip of the island for Puka Shell Beach – it's glorious!

3 → THE GAY SCENE OF MANILA

The largest gay scene in the country with popular clubs like O Bar and Adonis dominating the scene with drag shows and an array of exotic dancers. Nectar Nightclub is another popular gay club for lovers of electro music. For gay bars, we recommend the Bohemian vibe of Catch272 or the gay karaoke nights at Jefz Café. In terms of gay events, Metro Manila Pride in March is one of the largest in Asia. There is also a second smaller Pride event in Quezon City every December.

4 → UNDERGROUND RIVER NEAR PUERTO PRINCESA

One of the world's longest underground rivers at 8.2km (5.1 miles), surrounded by gorgeous limestone karsts. Every Filipino we met proudly reminded us that this is one of the New Seven Wonders of Nature!

5 → BEACH CAMPING ON CORON ISLAND

Coron Island in the Palawan Province is pretty remote and harder to reach than other places in Palawan, but is worth the trip. It is untouched and beautiful: this is the place to come to escape the world. Most head here via an internal flight from Manila to Busuanga and a short taxi ride to Coron Island. Otherwise, it's a fifteen-hour ferry from Manila or Puerta Princesa (the main town and transport hub of Palawan). From El Nido, it's a 4-hour ferry ride to Coron.

6 → TRY AN ALOHA BURGER AT JOLLIBEE

Jollibee is *the* ubiquitous fast food chain, known and loved by every Filipino everywhere. No trip to the Philippines is complete without trying a Tuna Pie or an Aloha Burger!

7 → ISLAND HOPPING ON A BANGKA BOAT

We'd never seen a boat like it before! They are like canoes, supported by two outriggers made from bamboo (called *katig*) on each side that stabilize the boat. We did several short trips from Palawan and Boracay on bangka boats.

8 → BATAD RICE TERRACES IN BANAUE

The views across this UNESCO World Heritage Site are stunning. The rice terraces cover around 10,360 sq km (4,000 sq miles) of steep, mountainous terrain in these intricate maze-like carved terraces, some of which are 2,000 years old. Most will arrange their visit via a local tour company from Manila; otherwise it's a nine-hour overnight bus ride.

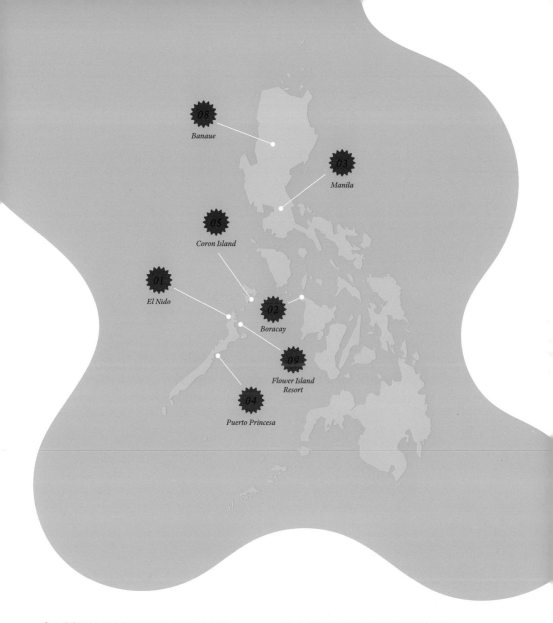

08 Banaue

03 Manila

05 Coron Island

01 El Nido

02 Boracay

09 Flower Island Resort

04 Puerto Princesa

9 → ROMANTIC SPLURGE AT FLOWER ISLAND RESORT

Our private island getaway in the middle of the Pacific Ocean, it was a one-hour speedboat ride from Palawan. It's completely isolated, surrounded by the most impressive coral reef we've ever seen. We stayed in our own luxurious private hut right on the beach. . . you just can't beat this!

10 → WE DARE YOU TO TRY BALUT!

This popular snack is a fertilized duck embryo that is roughly seventeen days old. It is boiled and the embryo eaten straight out of the shell. It's got a crunch! We tried it on Puka Shell Beach in Boracay from a street vendor who was selling them to local children.

OUR PRACTICAL TIPS FOR LGBTQ+ TRAVELLERS

The Philippines

1 → THE PHILIPPINES IS GAY-FRIENDLY

The Philippines is one of the more liberal-minded places we visited in Asia. We saw more openly gay and transgender people here than anywhere else on the continent, especially in Manila and Boracay.

2 → CATHOLICISM RULES THE SCHOOL

Despite its gay friendliness, the Philippines is super religious! Locals take great pride in Catholicism and society is quite conservative. We therefore advise erring on the side of caution when it comes to PDAs.

3 → BOOK A GAY-FRIENDLY HOTEL

Most places won't bat an eyelid at two men wanting to share a double bed. However, some family-run guesthouses may frown upon it. If booking at an international hotel like the Hyatt, Marriott, Sofitel, or the Hilton you won't have any problems at all, and we recommend these if you have any concerns. Alternatively, email/call your hotel beforehand to ask if they're OK to host a same-sex couple.

4 → THE FILIPINOS ARE SOME OF THE WARMEST PEOPLE ON THE PLANET

We're sure you'll also draw this conclusion. The Filipinos welcome foreigners with open arms and make a point of Filipino Hospitality. For example, if they invite you out, they will pay the bill. They want to do everything to make their guests feel welcome. This is one of the reasons we think the Philippines is one of the more gay-friendly places in Asia.

5 → MACHISMO CULTURE STILL PREVAILS

Whilst society is quickly changing its perception towards the LGBTQ+ community, large swathes of it still retain a strong "machismo" culture where men must "act like men", produce lots of babies, show no emotion, and so on.

→ **RESOURCES**

The British Foreign Office advice for the Philippines advises against all travel to Mindanao and the Sulu archipelago in the south because of clashes between military and insurgent groups. Check the latest advice from your local government before travelling.

LEFT Snorkelling in El Nido, Palawan Island.

Stefan

"UNDER THE SEA!"
The Philippines

"Seby, can you guess what I got you for your birthday present?"

*B*y this stage of our relationship, Seby knew that I love birthday present planning. I spend months in advance researching, trying to find him the most unexpected, random, out-of-the-ordinary gift.

So naturally, when I found out about mermaid classes in Boracay during our trip to the Philippines, I knew exactly what I was going to get him!

I strongly believe that inside every gay man lies a beautiful mermaid waiting to break out. Am I stereotyping too much? Then let me rephrase, inside these two travel queens are wannabe mermaids ready to take the centre stage. . .

Miss Ariel, honey, move aside cause the Nomadic Boys' Mermaids just sashayed into town!

The actual "town" is an island – Boracay. It's one of the prime tourist hotspots in the Philippines, famed for its colourful coral reefs, palm trees,

and sandy pristine beaches. It's also developed a reputation for being a party destination, particularly for the LGBTQ+ community. If you look beneath the surface of those cool, tranquil blue waters, you'll find an assortment of marine life, abandoned shipwrecks, and maybe even a mermaid or two. . .

Sightings of mermaids have been confirmed by multiple coastguards on the beach. . . but disappointingly, it's just people warming up their muscles and taking mermaid classes!

Mermaid School has become very fashionable in recent times. As well as in Boracay, we found mermaid schools in Gran Canaria, Florida, and Copenhagen – the latter even has a bronze statue devoted to *The Little Mermaid*.

We started off our mermaid class with our hot instructor David. I should point out at this stage that swimming with a monofin is pretty challenging; it requires a significant amount of body strength, particularly your core, so mermaid swimmers are *ripped!*

Hot David first took us through various warm up exercises to stretch out our muscles and prepare for swimming. Then, we slid into our foxy monofins. Mine, a dashing warm lavender, whilst Seby opted for a verdant green.

We served fish-*tastic* realness!

With our fins securely fastened, it was time to get into the water. Swimming like a mermaid is hard work. It's not for the faint-hearted. Hot David told us that our legs need to stay straight, and our arms locked stretched out in front of us. Getting into the perfect groove takes a bit of time, but once we got our bodies to move with a subtle ripple-like wave effect, we started to nail it.

Swimming like a mermaid is also about being graceful and elegant. Unfortunately, I looked more like a

~~~~~~~~~~~~~~~~~~~~~

I strongly believe that inside every gay man lies a beautiful mermaid waiting to break out.

~~~~~~~~~~~~~~~~~~~~~

clumsy whale trying to dive, but birthday boy Seby didn't fare too badly. He was living his best life, elegantly gliding through the water. Hot David was impressed by Seby as were the hordes of onlooking tourists watching, giggling at these two middle aged blokes living out their mermaid fantasy. . .

By the end of our mermaid swimming lesson, we were exhausted and welcomed the chance to just relax on the lovely White Beach of Boracay in the sunshine. I knew what I had to get Seby for next year's birthday: transformation into iconic Ursula Sea Witches.

↗ Asia

MONGOLIA

For gay travellers, Mongolia might not be the first choice, but it offers a unique and awe-inspiring experience.

1 → FAVOURITE GAY CLUB
Hanzo, Ulaanbaatar

2 → FAVOURITE FESTIVAL
Naadam opening ceremony in Ulaanbaatar in July

3 → FAVOURITE LANDSCAPE
Tsagaan Suvarga in the Gobi Desert

4 → FAVOURITE EXPERIENCE
Living with nomadic families in their yurts

5 → FAVOURITE FOOD
Khorkhog (Mongolian goat barbecue-cooked with hot stones)

*T*he most remarkable place we've ever been! Mongolia, the realm of Genghis Khan, is a landlocked country in Asia and home to one of the largest deserts in the world. There are more horses than people, and fermented horse milk (*airag*) is the drink of choice!

We visited Mongolia after our Trans-Siberian railway adventure finished. We didn't expect to end up staying for a month, but we were so fascinated by the humble lifestyle of the nomadic tribes living in the Mongolian steppe that we were eager to learn more about their lives.

Far from the vibrant circuit parties of Barcelona or the LGBTQ+ events of Palm Springs, Mongolia unveils otherworldly landscapes and a profound connection with nature.

That's not to say it's completely devoid of any gay life! There's a small gay scene in the capital, Ulaanbaatar, led by the country's sole gay bar, Hanzo. Every weekend, the local LGBTQ+ community of Ulaanbaatar gathers at Hanzo for a fun-filled evening of dancing, prancing, and plenty of gossiping!

LEFT Tsagaan Suvarga in the Gobi Desert.

OUR TOP EXPERIENCES
✈ *Mongolia*

1 → ATTEND THE MONGOLIAN OLYMPICS IN JULY

Held annually in Ulaanbaatar, it features a spectacular opening ceremony followed by three days of events: wrestling, archery, and horse-riding. We got our tickets for the Opening Ceremony via Sunpath Hostel.

2 → WATCH THE ALTAI GOLDEN EAGLE FESTIVAL

On the first weekend of October in the Bayan-Ölgii province, Kazakh eagle hunters compete in this festival. Prizes are awarded for speed, agility, accuracy, and for the best traditional Kazakh dress. The festival was featured in the 2016 movie *The Eagle Huntress*.

3 → VISIT HANZO – THE ONLY (KNOWN) GAY BAR IN MONGOLIA

The owner, Zorig, is a formidable member of the country's LGBTQ+ community who has owned and run a gay bar in Ulaanbaatar for decades. He changes its name and location every few years to keep patrons safe. When we visited, it was located near the main railway station of Ulaanbaatar.

4 → EQUALITY WALK IN AUGUST

Every August, the LGBTQ+ community of Ulaanbaatar has a Pride event called the Equality Walk. As well as a parade through the city's downtown area, it also features a public concert, film festival, and then concludes at Zorig's gay bar Hanzo for a Pride-themed after party.

5 → EXPLORE THE GOBI DESERT ON A TOUR

The largest desert in Asia. We loved the variety of landscapes: one day we'd be riding camels through the long stretches of sand, the next day we were exploring the fiery red rocks of the Bayanzag Flaming Cliffs, and the following day we were hiking through the stunning Tsagaan Suvarga mine (a prehistoric seabed). The Gobi Desert is sure to inspire many photographers!

6 → LIVE WITH NOMADS IN THEIR YURTS

During our Gobi Desert tour, we stayed with nomad families in their *gers* (yurts) every night. They gave us an insight into their day-to-day lives, such as what they eat and how everything is made – everything is home-grown. We also learnt about their different customs and traditions, which date back

→ **WE CHALLENGE YOU TO TRY *AIRAG*!**

A fermented mare's milk with an alcoholic content of around 2–3%. Upon entering a nomadic family's ger, it's traditional for guests to be offered a bowl of airag to share. It's considered an insult to refuse, so we were encouraged to at least take a few sips.

The taste? Like a sharp, strong yogurt drink that's long passed its expiry date. . . A few sips of it and we were only too happy to pass the bowl on to the next person. It eventually circled back to our host who, while we looked on in amazement, enthusiastically gulped down the entire bowl!

05

to the days of Genghis Khan. It's a simple, humble way of life. No Wi-Fi out here!

7 → SEE WILD HORSES IN HUSTAI NATIONAL PARK

Mongolia is the only place in the world where you can see wild *takhi* horses. They are stockier compared to domesticated horses, with shorter legs. *Takhi* means "spirit" in Mongolian and they are considered a symbol of national heritage. The park is around two-to-three hours' drive from Ulaanbaatar.

8 → KHARKHORUM AND THE ORKHON VALLEY

The Orkhon Valley has an abundance of archaeological remains dating back to the 6th century. The one we were most excited to see was the site of the historic city Kharkhorum, established by Genghis Kahn in 1220 and which later became the capital of the Mongol Empire.

9 → MONGOLIAN THROAT SINGING

Khöömei is a traditional singing style in Mongolia where singers use a form of circular breathing which allows them to sustain multiple notes for long periods of time. We watched one of our nomadic hosts perform it live to calm his camels and put them to sleep. . . all with the backdrop of the sun setting over the Gobi Desert!

Every August, the LGBTQ+ community of Ulaanbaatar has a Pride event called *the Equality Walk*. As well as a parade through the city's downtown area, it also features a public concert, film festival, and then concludes at Zorig's gay bar Hanzo for a *Pride-themed* after party!

OUR PRACTICAL TIPS FOR LGBTQ+ TRAVELLERS

Mongolia

1 → GAY-FRIENDLY, BUT. . .

As gay tourists visiting Mongolia, we found it to be safe. Mongolians we met were more curious about where we're from rather than our relationship. However, this is more down to the fact that as a foreigner you get a sort of "pass" that sadly the local LGBTQ+ community doesn't get to enjoy.

2 → MONGOLIAN SOCIETY IS CONSERVATIVE

It is so conservative that most gay guys stay in the closet. Our friend Zorig told us that the biggest problem he has running a gay bar in Ulaanbaatar was not the homophobia from the local council or police but trying to convince the local LGBTQ+ community to visit and support it – most were too scared to be seen in public at a gay place.

3 → BOOKING HOTEL ROOMS WAS NOT A PROBLEM

When it came to booking accommodation, we never had any problems booking a double bed. The guesthouses and hotels we stayed at in Ulaanbaatar were absolutely fine about this. Our tour guides knew we were gay but didn't bat an eyelid, though this is more likely because we were tourists. In any case, all the yurts we stayed in featured only single beds for guests.

4 → CAUTION WITH PDAS

We were careful not to throw our relationship in people's faces, especially when staying with the nomadic families. We avoided expressing affection towards each other in public unless we knew we were in a gay-friendly space such as an international bar or at Zorig's gay bar.

5 → HIRE A DRIVER AND A GUIDE

Trips around Mongolia require a strong and hardy 4x4, a knowledgeable local driver, and ideally a guide. Outside of Ulaanbaatar there are few roads, mainly dirt tracks. All hotels will be linked to a tour company and can arrange everything for you. We arranged all our tours via Sunpath Hostel.

6 → GAY TOURS IN MONGOLIA

There are two gay tours that take place every year. The first is with HE Travel in July which coincides with the Naadam Festival. The second is with Out Adventures in October, which takes place during the Golden Eagle Festival.

RIGHT Goats roaming free in the Orkhon Valley in Central Mongolia.

Asia

NEPAL

For us, Nepal was a dream – and our ultimate trekking destination. The allure of Nepal's majestic beauty calls us back time and again!

1 → FAVOURITE TREK
Annapurna Circuit to Thorong La pass

2 → FAVOURITE GAY BAR
PINK Tiffany in Thamel, Kathmandu

3 → FAVOURITE FOOD
Dal bhat

4 → FAVOURITE LANDSCAPE
Sunrise at Poon Hill, Gandaki Province

5 → FAVOURITE MEMORY
Sailing on Phewa Lake, Pokhara

"Nepal is like a drug for trekkers! Trust me boys, after your first Himalayan adventure, you'll be racing to your laptop to book your next trip!"

That's what our friend told us in the taxi we shared together from Kathmandu airport. *This was his 13th visit!*

With the world's tallest mountain, Everest, and around 75% of its landscape adorned with dramatic peaks, Nepal offers every trekkie endless exploration that could span a lifetime.

And if that wasn't enough, Nepal is gay-friendly! It has some of the most progressive LGBTQ+ laws in Asia. For example, after Nepal decriminalized homosexuality in 2007, it proceeded to recognize LGBTQ+ rights as fundamental rights in its constitution. In 2011, it made history by including a third gender on its federal census – a global first! Recently, in 2023, the Supreme Court ordered the recognition of same-sex marriages.

And sure enough, as our friend predicted, we're already planning our return trip!

LEFT View of the Himalayas from Yak Kharkha during the Annapurna Trek.

OUR TOP EXPERIENCES
⟁ *Nepal*

1 → CLIMB TO EVEREST BASE CAMP

One for the bucket list! The highest mountain in the world is located at an altitude of 5,364m (17,598ft). Along the way you visit monasteries, Buddhist stupas, colourful prayer flags, and traverse along metal bridges strung across deep canyons. Of course, you also gain bragging rights for having accomplished one of the most famous treks in the world!

02

2 → TREK THE ANNAPURNA CIRCUIT TO THORONG LA PASS

In our opinion, this is the Mother of all Himalayan hikes! The entire trek is around 230km (145 miles) and usually takes ten days. At 5,416m (17,762ft), it is one of the highest passes in the world. During your trek, you stay overnight at local Himalayan teahouses run by locals, which is a cultural experience in its own right.

3 → THE GAY SCENE OF KATHMANDU

Thamel is the touristic heart of Kathmandu with the best restaurants, hotels, and bars. PINK Tiffany is the main LGBTQ+ hangout. There are a handful of other gay-friendly places which, on occasion, host an LGBTQ+ night like Fire Club, Tom And Jerry Pub, and Purple Haze Rock Bar.

4 → GO BACK IN TIME TO BHAKTAPUR

This UNESCO-listed city is one of the prettiest places in Nepal, famed for its rich cultural heritage, architecture, craft, and artworks. It's on the east corner of Kathmandu Valley, making it an ideal day trip from the capital. Walking around Bhaktapur felt like we'd been teleported back to ancient times!

5 → NEPAL PRIDE PARADE

This is held annually on the second Saturday of June in Kathmandu. There are other ad hoc LGBTQ+ events that take place throughout the year organized by the Blue Diamond Society (see page 110).

6 → GO ON SAFARI IN CHITWAN NATIONAL PARK

An incredible spot in Nepal to see wildlife including Bengal tigers, Indian leopards, sloth bears, otters, foxes, honey badgers, rhinos, and elephants. Established in 1973, it was Nepal's first National Park, which then subsequently became a UNESCO World Heritage Site.

7 → GET SOME R&R IN POKHARA

Nepal's second-largest city is a treat. Whereas Kathmandu is a buzzing metropolis, Pokhara feels chilled in comparison. We spent the day here after our Annapurna Trek and we rented a boat to sail along the Phewa Lake. One site we loved was the Shanti Stupa – a Buddhist shrine on the Anadu Hill.

02 *Annapurna Circuit*

03 *Kathmandu*

01 *Everest Base Camp*

07 *Pokhara*

06 *Chitwan National Park*

09 *Chandragiri Hills*

04 *Bhaktapur*

8 → TRY SOME NEPALESE FOOD

Dal bhat is the national dish, comprising of various curries (usually lentil-based) with rice. During our Annapurna Trek, we would eat it twice a day. Our guide would jokingly say: "Dal bhat power, 24 hour!" Other Nepalese culinary highlights we loved include *momos* (dumplings), *sel roti* (sweet pastries), *dhindo* (flour-based pudding), *gundruk* (fermented vegetables), and *kheer* (rice pudding).

9 → ENJOY THE VIEW AT CHANDRAGIRI HILLS

It's an hour southwest of Kathmandu, ideal for a day trip. On a clear day, you can see both the Annapurna mountain and Mount Everest. It's not too strenuous and there is a cable car to whisk you to the top where we recommend exploring the Bhaleshwor Mahadev temple.

OUR PRACTICAL TIPS FOR LGBTQ+ TRAVELLERS

⌐ Nepal

1 → NEPAL IS GAY-FRIENDLY

We felt welcome travelling as a gay couple in Nepal. We never had problems getting a double bed. The people were welcoming and friendly, and curious to know more about us. Although for LGBTQ+ locals, things are different. Nepal is socially conservative.

2 → ORGANIZE YOUR TREK IN KATHMANDU

Thamel in Kathmandu is an awesome base, and is worth spending a few days in. For independent travellers, we recommend organizing your trek here so that you can meet your guide before committing to anything. You will be spending two weeks together in close quarters, so you ideally want someone you'll vibe with.

3 → GAY TOURS IN NEPAL

There are a handful of gay tour companies offering trips to Nepal. The main ones are Out Adventures, who lead a tour to Everest Base Camp every October and November, and Brand g Vacations who combine Nepal with Bhutan (also in October) for a unique trip through the Himalayas.

4 → ALTITUDE SICKNESS

This is a big deal, especially when you're trekking upwards of 2,000m (6,562ft). We started to feel it strongly from around 4,500m (14,764ft). Symptoms included headaches and exhaustion after taking a few short steps! Take it slow, and give your body enough time to acclimatize by starting at a lower altitude and ascending each day by around 500–1,000m (1,640–3,281ft).

→ **FAMOUS OUT AND PROUD NEPALESE LGBTQ+ PEOPLE**

Meghna Lama is a transgender fashion model who set up the PINK Tiffany gay parties in Kathmandu. Sunil Babu Pant was the first openly gay federal legislator in not only Nepal, but in the whole of Asia! In 2001, he also formed the Blue Diamond Society, an organization that advocates for the rights of LGBTQ+ people in Nepal. Bhumika Shrestha is an actor and third gender activist, who also works with the Blue Diamond Society. Also, be sure to check out the 2011 film Snow Flower and the Secret Fan about two women in love but unable to come out and be together – it's often nicknamed "Brokeback Everest".

With the world's *tallest* mountain, Everest, and around 75% of its landscape adorned with *dramatic* peaks, Nepal offers every trekkie *endless* exploration that could span a lifetime. And if that wasn't enough, Nepal is gay-friendly!

"GASPING FOR BREATH"
⬈ *Nepal*

On one of our treks, altitude sickness quickly set in!

"*Stefan! Wake up – I can't breathe. I need help!*"

We had settled into High Camp, a guesthouse for trekkers nestled at a daunting 4,800m (15,748ft) high. Today marked our momentous ascent to Thorong La pass, the climax of our Annapurna Trek, standing tall at a staggering 5,416m (17,769ft).

However, this was also the moment the altitude sickness struck with a vengeance!

Frantically, I managed to find the Coca-Cola bottle our guide had advised us to drink when experiencing any symptoms of altitude sickness. Miraculously, it worked and I was able to go back to sleep for a bit...

At around 4:30a.m. our guide woke us up, urging us to pack our things quickly so we could set off at 5a.m.

The reason for the early start was to avoid the strong winds that pick up in the late morning at Thorong La pass,

I couldn't help the tears that came streaming down my face. They were tears of joy mixed with so much emotion.

Struggling to draw a complete breath, I felt a relentless, throbbing headache that jolted me awake at 3:30a.m. These were common symptoms, but they caught me off guard while I was asleep, fuelling panic.

Despite my distress, Stefan remained fast asleep and snored loudly, exhausted from the previous day's trek.

which can become treacherous. We heard stories of people getting stuck there and freezing to death!

We set off. We only had to trek up 616m (2,021ft) from High Camp to Thorong La pass, but the altitude sickness made it seem like we were doing a marathon. At this high altitude, our bodies were working overtime.

I could feel my heart racing, my head was pounding, and I was constantly *starving*!

We progressed slowly, pausing frequently to catch our breath, sipping Coca-Cola to alleviate the headaches, and relishing the snacks Stefan had stashed away in his backpack.

To add to the challenge, the biting cold was unrelenting. The woolly hats, gloves, and down jackets we hastily purchased in Kathmandu before our trek proved to be our saviours. Taking off my gloves to capture a photo felt as though my fingers would freeze off each time.

Thankfully, the excitement of reaching the peak fuelled our adrenaline, allowing us to plough on.

By around 7:30a.m. we reached the climax of the Annapurna Trek: Thorong La pass.

It felt glorious!

And the views around us were *breathtaking*!

For starters, we were *above* the clouds. It was like I was in the heavens peering down on Planet Earth. All around me I could see snow-capped mountain peaks poking out through the ethereal cloud forest. My heart was pumping fast, only this time it was from the rush of excitement I was feeling standing there, high above the rest of the world with my Stefan next to me who was also looking out in awe.

I couldn't help the tears that came streaming down my face. They were tears of joy mixed with so much emotion. It had been a challenging morning with little sleep and one of the most intense experiences of my life. At one point, I doubted if I would make it!

And yet, it was worth every second.

And I craved more! I wanted to rush back to my laptop to book our next Himalayan adventure. Yup, our friend wasn't wrong!

⤴ Asia

LAOS

We knew so little about this hidden gem and yet to say we were blown away would be an understatement!

1 → FAVOURITE GAY BAR
The Lao Café (CCC Bar), Vientiane

2 → FAVOURITE LANDSCAPE
Kuang Si Falls

3 → FAVOURITE ACTIVITY
The Living Land Farm, Luang Prabang

4 → FAVOURITE FOOD
Laab (raw minced meat salad)

5 → TOP CHILL OUT
Sailing on the Mekong River

One moment that stands out for us was during our day trip to the alluring Kuang Si Waterfall near Luang Prabang, the view of which gifted us an unforgettable photo that now proudly adorns our living room wall – a testament to its beauty.

Laos, a landlocked country in southeast Asia, shares its borders with China to the North, Myanmar to the northwest, Thailand to the southwest, Cambodia to the south, and Vietnam to the east. Each neighbour has influenced Laos, forging strong cultural ties over time. Notably, the French colonial period, from 1893 to 1953, has also left a lasting mark.

The country even has its own unique beer called Beerlao. It is made from rice instead of malt because barley does not grow as effectively as rice does in Laos. Rice is the main agricultural produce here. Beerlao is super refreshing, especially when served ice cold. . . *Thum keo* ("cheers" in Lao)!

As a gay couple exploring Laos, we encountered no issues. Laotians are relaxed, tolerant, and respectful people who embraced us wholeheartedly.

RIGHT Diving with young monks at the Kuang Si Falls, Luang Prabang.

OUR TOP EXPERIENCES
✈ *Laos*

1 → KUANG SI FALLS
A stunning three-tiered waterfall located 29km (18 miles) south of Luang Prabang in the middle of a jungle. The best part is you can hike to the top and then swim in the pristine water created by the cascades – a welcome respite from the hot and humid climate.

2 → LUANG PRABANG OLD TOWN
The former royal capital of Laos until 1975, the district is now a charming UNESCO-listed place to visit. Despite being touristy, it has retained its authentic charm. We loved visiting its bustling markets, and also the Buddhist temples such as the gilded Wat Xieng Thong (which dates back to the 1500s).

3 → THE GAY SCENE OF VIENTIANE
The capital city, Vientiane, is where we found the largest LGBTQ+ community. The Lao Café (CCC Bar) is the only official gay bar in the entire country that we could find.

4 → NIGHT MARKET OF LUANG PRABANG
Every evening stroll through the streets of Luang Prabang was a joy! From around 6p.m., rows of stalls would sell freshly-made barbecued meats, noodle soups, spicy papaya salads, coconut pancakes, and sticky rice treats. It would satisfy the curiosity of any foodie!

5 → THE LIVING LAND FARM IN LUANG PRABANG
A half-day experience where local farmers take you through the different stages of rice production, which included Stefan ploughing a field with a water buffalo called Suzuki. Not only is it educational, but you get to support the local community.

6 → TAKE A COOKING CLASS AT TAMARIND RESTAURANT
One of the most highly-rated restaurants in Luang Prabang, it hosts daily cooking classes. They taught us to make various Laotian dishes including *mok pa* (fish steamed in banana leaves), stuffed lemongrass chicken, and coconut sticky rice. To this day, we still use our Tamarind cooking book that they gave us as a souvenir!

7 → SAIL ON THE MEKONG RIVER
The main river that runs through Laos. It starts in Tibet and then snakes its way through China, Myanmar, Laos, Thailand, Cambodia, and Vietnam. Many companies offer river cruises along parts of the Mekong River which can be anything from half a day to two weeks long.

8 → VISIT THE COPE VISITOR CENTRE IN VIENTIANE
During the Vietnam War, the USA dropped 2.5 million tons of explosives on Laos. Many of these remained unexploded, and have exploded on innocent victims who, years later, stumbled on them by accident. COPE serves to support them and tell their story.

9 → TRY SOME LAOTIAN FOOD!
Laab is the most famous Laotian dish, and it's a minced meat salad often served raw – the meat cooks in a lime and spice juice. Rice is a staple in Laos, especially sticky rice. Other Laotian foods we love include *sai kok* (spicy sausage), *tam mak hoong* (spicy papaya salad), and baguette sandwiches (an influence from the days of French colonization).

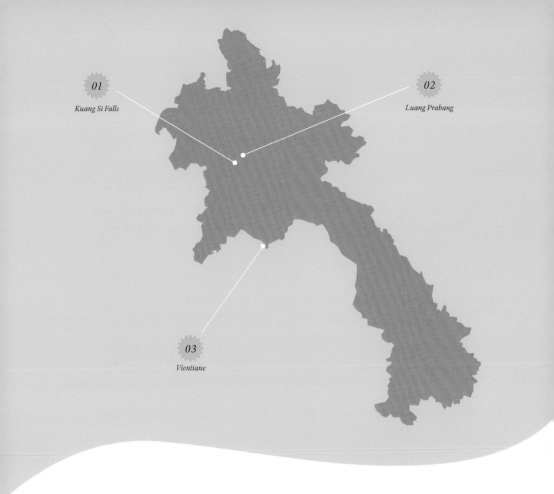

01 *Kuang Si Falls*

02 *Luang Prabang*

03 *Vientiane*

OUR PRACTICAL TIPS FOR LGBTQ+ TRAVELLERS

1 → LAOS IS VERY SAFE

We never faced any difficulties in Laos. The people are peaceful and avoid conflict. They are respectful and welcoming to foreigners. Violent crime is low compared to other parts of Asia that we visited. We never felt uneasy anywhere nor had any problems booking a double bed in any of the hotels or guesthouses we stayed.

2 → LAOTIAN SOCIETY IS CONSERVATIVE

Despite feeling safe in Laos as a gay couple, we do need to stress that society is conservative. We get a *pass* to be ourselves as we are foreigners, but for locals, the situation is different. Whilst being gay is legal, there are no anti-discrimination laws to protect the LGBTQ+ community and same-sex unions or marriages are not recognized. . . *yet*! As such, quite a few of the gay locals we met felt they had to lead a closeted life.

Stefan

"HERE GOES NOTHING!"

✈ *Laos*

Written in loving memory of our dear friend, Somphorn Boupha who sadly passed away from cancer in June 2019.

"Hop on guys. I've packed us a chilled case of beers that has been sitting in my freezer all night."

It was a bright Sunday morning in Luang Prabang when our friend, Somphorn, picked us up in his car. We met Somphorn the night before in the gay-friendly bar Lao Lao Gardens (now permanently closed). He was the bar's owner, and was excited to show us around.

The night before, he had taken us to various bars where we'd made a whole heap of new friends including a few gay travellers who Somphorn had also connected with earlier that evening. Towards the end of the night, Somphorn had suggested that our little gay group visit the Kuang Si Falls together the following day and he would be only too happy to take us. We jumped at the chance!

"I'm more a Gin and Dubonnet kind of gal, Somphorn, but chilled beers will do me fine" – my Seby always trying to keep it classy. . .

Once inside Somphorn's car, we left the city and drove for around fifty minutes through the picturesque countryside of Luang Prabang until we reached the Kuang Si Falls. We left the car in the parking area and then grabbed our rucksacks for the short twenty-minute trek to the falls.

We eventually caught up with Somphorn and his friends who had already reached the lower waterfall pool area.

By this point we were parched and dripping with sweat. We were only too happy to go straight in the refreshing water to cool down.

Suddenly we heard a splash! Then another. . . *followed by another.*

We looked up and saw red blurs of colour falling through the sky into the water next to us! It was a group of young monks dressed in their striking scarlet robes jumping from the tiers above. As it was a Sunday, the young monks were permitted a day off to visit the Falls.

Taking Somphorn's lead, we climbed up to the top of the cascades so we

could also jump down the waterfall into the refreshing pool of water below. At the top we had a glorious 360-degree view of the thick jungle we'd just hiked through. *It was quite something.* As far as my eye could see, we were surrounded by dense vegetation.

Waiting in line behind the monks, we watched as each person went to the edge and then leapt out into the air, dropping several metres into the pool of water below.

It was beautiful, because it captured a wonderful memory that we all shared together.

Although, I have a fear of heights – jumping out into a large pool of water from a significant height puts the fear of God in me!

"Come on, Stefan. If young teenage monks can do it, then you'll be just fine!"

Seby had a point. Watching the young kids cry out with joy as they leapt out and dropped into the pool of water below did help alleviate my fears.

Together, Seby and I crept to the edge.

"I'll count to 3, and then we'll jump," I said. *"Ok, Stefan? 3. . . 2. . . 1. . ."*

Then out we leapt.

Adrenaline coursed through my body as we descended and splashed into the pool of water below.

As we came up for breath, the young monks were pointing, smiling, and clapping at us. Somphorn rushed over to show us the picture he'd taken.

It was beautiful, because it captured a wonderful memory that we all shared together.

Today, that same photo now hangs proudly on our living room wall back home and reminds us of our dearly departed friend, Somphorn Boupha. RIP. Somphorn was a stalwart figure in the LGBTQ+ community of Laos and his memory will forever live on in our hearts.

SOUTH AMERICA

We could happily spend a lifetime exploring South America. For starters, it's *rich with unique otherworldly sites* and landscapes, like Machu Picchu in Peru, Perito Moreno Glacier in Argentina, the Atacama Desert in North Chile, Cocora Valley in Colombia – we could go on for hours listing them. . .

It's also a *paradise for wildlife lovers* – the Amazon Rainforest, the Galápagos Islands in Ecuador, Penïnsula Valdés in Argentina. . . Then there's the *epic treks* like Torres del Paine in Chile, El Chaltén in Argentina, and the Mother of all treks, the Inca Trail in Peru.

Most importantly of all, the bulk of South America is gay-friendly. For years, Argentina, Brazil, Uruguay, Colombia, Chile, and Ecuador have been *spearheading LGBTQ+ rights*, each passing gay marriage laws. Lagging behind them are the more conservative Peru, Bolivia, Paraguay, and Venezuela. The *largest gay Pride* in the world? That's in São Paolo, Brazil. The largest gay club on the continent? That'll be Theatron in Bogotá, Colombia. Trust us, you'll have a lot of fun here!

ARGENTINA

There's nothing more intimate than dancing the tango in the embrace of your lover, moving together in time to the music.

1 → FAVOURITE BRUNCH SPOT
Pride Café, San Telmo, Buenos Aires

2 → FAVOURITE SUNDAY MARKET
Feria de San Telmo, Buenos Aires

3 → FAVOURITE HIKE
Laguna de Los Tres, El Chaltén

4 → FAVOURITE FOODS
The steak! Also, try the empanadas, milanesas, and provoleta cheese.

5 → FAVOURITE DRINK
Malbec, of course!

We were at our first queer tango class in a milonga (tango hall) in Buenos Aires. Although total beginners, we managed to pick up the basic moves so that we could continue dancing freestyle after class had finished.

Boy was it romantic! Like nothing else we'd experienced before. The sounds of the tango music made us feel like we'd been transported to another era: the distinct accented staccato, the sudden changes in dynamics, and the melancholic sounds from the bandoneon accordion.

We've been to Argentina several times, each time exploring a different corner of the country. It's massive, but what a joy to explore. There's so much to see and do. But our main take away is how gay-friendly Argentina is!

LEFT Fitz Roy mountain view, El Chaltén.

OUR TOP EXPERIENCES

Argentina

1 → THE GAY SCENE OF BUENOS AIRES

Palermo is the main gay area, with a large LGBTQ+ community. The gay hangouts we liked the most were Peuteo, km Zero, Glam Disco, Amerika, and Contramano.

2 → QUEER TANGO CLASS, BUENOS AIRES

Some of the milongas in Buenos Aires host a queer tango class like LA MarSHàlL Milonga. Look out for the Tango Queer Festivals that take place in Buenos Aires. The dates are not fixed but in recent years they took place in February and November.

3 → HIKE PERITO MORENO GLACIER

This huge ice formation is 35km (22 miles) in length – the size of Buenos Aires city, with a depth of up to 180m (590ft). You're only allowed to do this as part of a supervised tour, which is easy to arrange in the nearby town of El Calafate. At the end of our tour, our guide whipped out some whisky and a couple of glasses, and poured us a drink served with fresh ice cut directly from the glacier!

4 → WHALE WATCHING IN PUERTO MADRYN

June to December is the whale watching season in Puerto Madryn. Whilst most whale watching happens by boat, sometimes you can spot the whales from La Rambla – the city's seafront promenade.

5 → MARCHA DEL ORGULLO, BUENOS AIRES

This is Buenos Aires' gay pride parade that takes place every November. It's one of the largest in South America attracting around 200,000 people.

6 → VENDIMIA GAY WINE HARVESTING FESTIVAL, MENDOZA

Wine tasting in the bodegas of Mendoza is a must. If visiting in March, check out the LGBTQ+ "Vendimia Para Todos" (Vendimia for everyone) festival. It's part of the annual Grape Harvest Festival, which includes a colourful parade of the "Vendimia Queens", and a concert featuring a Drag Queen beauty contest.

→ **DID YOU KNOW?**

The tango was originally a dance between two men, beginning in the lower-class immigrant communities of Buenos Aires in the 1870s. These communities were male-dominated. Famines were ravishing Europe at the time, so families sent their sons to the Americas. Due to the shortage of women, men in these communities would dance together to brush up their moves. . . the tango is quite an intimate dance, so you can just imagine the homoerotic vibe amongst these young, virile men, right? Escándalo!

07 → Iguazu Falls

06 → Mendoza

09 → Esteros del Iberá wetland

01 → Buenos Aires

04 → Puerto Madryn

08 → El Chaltén

03 → Perito Moreno Glacier

7 → MARVEL AT THE IGUAZU FALLS

Often lauded as the world's most spectacular waterfall. We certainly thought so! As did UNESCO, and also the voters of the New Seven Wonders of Nature competition! You can't beat the power and raw beauty of Iguazu Falls.

8 → HIKING IN EL CHALTÉN

Our top trekking experience in Argentina. El Chaltén is a small town in the Santa Cruz region of Argentina, close to the Chilean border. It is surrounded by many trails. Our favourite was the trek to Laguna de Los Tres: we think that the views of Fitz Roy Mountain and the surrounding Andes mountain range are truly spectacular!

9 → THE ESTEROS DEL IBERÁ WETLAND

The second-largest wetland in the world, located in the province of Corrientes in northeast Argentina. Rich with wildlife, our highlight was taking a boat out to the middle of a lagoon to spot caimans in the wild.

ECUADOR

We've wanted to visit the Galápagos Islands for years, and when we did, it truly exceeded all our expectations!

1 → FAVOURITE GAY BAR

Kika in Quito, Ecuador

2 → SCARIEST MEMORY

Jumping into a piranha-infested waters of the Amazon Rainforest!

3 → FAVOURITE BEACH

Gardner Bay on Española Island in the Galápagos

4 → FAVOURITE FOOD

Locro de papa

5 → FAVOURITE MEMORY

Swimming with sea lion pups in the Galápagos

*T*he Galápagos Islands, with their captivating beauty and unique wildlife, left us in awe. However, we were pleasantly surprised to discover that Ecuador had so much more to offer beyond these enchanting islands. The country's diverse landscapes, from the dramatic Andes Mountains to the inviting beaches and the lush Amazon Rainforest, offered us a tapestry of unforgettable experiences.

Ecuador is also gay-friendly. In 2019, the introduction of gay marriage marked a momentous step forward for equality, while the existence of LGBTQ+ anti-discrimination laws since 1998 showcased the country's longstanding commitment to inclusivity. Ecuador's tourism industry, coupled with its close ties to the USA, has made it a popular destination for gay expats.

Throughout our time in Ecuador, we felt completely at ease and accepted, never encountering any obstacles or challenges.

→ SOME GAY ECUADORIAN SLANG OUR FRIENDS IN QUITO TAUGHT US

– Y la queso: *a phrase that has no meaning, but you'd use it, say, after making a sassy comment and snapping your fingers three times side to side as if to say "burrrn!"*

– Hola ñaña: *is like "hey gurrl" – ñaña is originally an indigenous Kichwa word meaning "sister".*

– Que fuerte: *has many meanings from "That's so huge!" to "That's so wrong!" or "That's so good!"*

– Querida: *means "Darling!" (imagine Lisa Vanderpump on The Real Housewives of Beverly Hills).*

– Chichis: *means "boobies" and is used colloquially by gay guys in Quito.*

OUR TOP EXPERIENCES

1 → THE GALÁPAGOS ISLANDS
Where Darwin wrote *On the Origin of Species* and home to over 9,000 wildlife species – many of which are found nowhere else in the world! There are a handful of companies that offer gay trips to the Galápagos, such as HE Travel and Out Adventures – be sure to check their websites for tour dates.

2 → GO ISLAND-HOPPING
Local gay-owned and gay-friendly companies that offer more exclusive gay charters to the Galápagos include Ecuador Nomadic. These enable you to visit the more remote islands at your leisure and stay near them overnight. If you're on a budget, you can instead base yourself on the main island, Santa Cruz, and visit the other islands via the public ferry. However, you'll have to return to Santa Cruz before nightfall, limiting your time exploring each island.

3 → GO WILDLIFE-WATCHING
We saw giant tortoises, land iguanas, marine iguanas, penguins, *oh so many different* birds, turtles, flamingos, sharks, and manta rays. We were also awestruck by incredible landscapes crafted by years of volcanic eruptions and tectonic plate movements.

4 → THE GAY SCENE OF QUITO
As well as being a charming city to explore (particularly the old town), the Ecuadorian capital has a bustling gay scene that comes alive at the weekends. Our favourite gay clubs to party in are Kika, El Hueco (also known as Tercer Milenio), and La Disco Bitch.

5 → FEEL THE SEA BREEZE AT MONTAÑITA
A coastal town with a Bohemian and liberal vibe, it's the most popular holiday destination in Ecuador for the LGBTQ+ community who head here to party at the Merman Beach Club and Poco Loco.

6 → EXPLORE THE AMAZON RAINFOREST
The gay-friendly Sacha Lodge is our top pick for an authentic and rustic jungle experience. It's hidden away, only accessible by boat. They offer a range of excursions including caiman spotting, kayaking, and jungle trekking. We even jumped into a lake full of piranhas – yikes!

7 → SWING OUT INTO THE ANDES MOUNTAINS IN BAÑOS
The El Vuelo del Condor (translates to "the flight of the condor") is located just outside Baños, perched up at 2,591m (8,500ft) in the Andes. It is a swing attached to two trees. Secured with a safety harness, you're then released to swing out over the mountains - let's just say that the views are just as impressive as the intense rush of adrenaline! Be warned, *you will shit yourself*!

8 → TRY SOME ECUADORIAN FOOD
How about some *llapingachos*? That's the most famous dish – fried stuffed potato patties. Others include: *locro de papa* (a potato-based soup), *hornado* (roasted pig), *fritada de chancho* (braised pork dish), and *seco de chivo* (goat stew). All washed down with a few *canelazos* – a warm cinnamon-spiced based Ecuadorian cocktail.

"WILL YOU PLAY WITH US, HOOMAN?"

↗ Ecuador

We had an incredible experience with sea lions in the Galápagos!

Sea lion babies are the puppies of the ocean. They swim all day long, playing and chasing each other in the water. Then, they head to the beach to dry off, posing in the sunshine as if begging to be photographed by adoring tourists like us: *not too dissimilar to my Stefan when he hits the beach in his tight white Speedos. . .*

The standout highlight for us in the Galápagos Islands was the sea lion pups. I have never seen anything cuter in my life.

Every day we would snorkel around the islands and the resident sea lion pups would always swim out to investigate us.

A strict rule is enforced in the Galápagos – you must stay at least 2 metres distance from all wildlife. But with the sea lion pups, this rule goes flying out the window. They don't care for human rules! They are so curious that they'd swim right up to us, nibble at our fins, as if begging us to come and play with them.

On our third day snorkelling, we spotted a small colony of sea lions swimming by the rocks. We carefully approached to investigate. Two of the colony's pups came over and started to dance around us. I swam with them, doing loops in the water. They swam down to pick up an unassuming sea cucumber and, using their snouts, they passed the poor sea cucumber to each other – as if playing volleyball!

At one point, one of the pups tossed the sea cucumber over to me. I was

startled! *What do I do?* The two pups just looked at me expectantly waiting for my reaction.

I realized they just wanted me to join in, so I carefully passed the sea cucumber back to one of them. I could have sworn he giggled as he received it from me!

moments from our travels come from interactions we have with locals, however in the uninhabited islands of the Galápagos, those locals are not humans, but sea lion pups. They welcomed us to their land and captivated us with their curiosity!

The standout highlight for us in the Galápagos Islands was the sea lion pups. I have never seen anything cuter!

The pups continued playing with the sea cucumber while doing loops around us in the water, but we had to eventually leave them to return to the boat.

What an epic afternoon!

Usually, our most memorable

They even waved us off as our plane left the tarmac at Baltra airport on our final day... *although that could have also been the effect of drinking one too many canelazos before boarding. Either way, sea lion pups rock!*

PERU

"We made it!" we proudly exclaimed to each other as we stood atop Huayna Picchu, gazing down at the ancient Incan city.

1 → BEST GAY BAR
Open Deck in
Miraflores, Lima

2 → FAVOURITE HIKE
Huayna Picchu at
Machu Picchu

**3 → FAVOURITE
COCKTAIL (EVER)**
Pisco sour

4 → FAVOURITE FOOD
Ceviche

**5 → MOST RELAXING
MEMORY**
Watching the sunset
over Lake Titicaca
from Amantaní Lodge

*T*his moment marked the pinnacle of our intense four-day hike up the Inca Trail to Machu Picchu in the Sacred Valley. Throughout the trek, we had our fair share of bickering, endured the lack of showers, braved sleeping in tents (*Stefan snored the loudest out of everybody!*), battled utter exhaustion, and endured continuous rain. . . And yet, we relished every single moment of this unforgettable journey!

This was our most cherished memory from Peru. Every morning we passed snow-capped mountain peaks, cloud forests, and Incan ruins. The trek finished at Machu Picchu: standing proud at 2,430m (7,972ft) altitude, it was built by the Incan Empire back in the 15th century and is considered to be their most impressive creation.

Beyond the awe-inspiring Machu Picchu, Peru has so much more to offer. From the dense wonders of the Amazon Rainforest to the rich tapestry of Incan culture in Cusco; from a tantalizing array of culinary delights to the budding gay scene in the capital Lima. Peru is ready to ignite your soul's wanderlust!

LEFT Llamas happily grazing away at Machu Picchu.

OUR TOP EXPERIENCES

✈ *Peru*

1 → REACH MACHU PICCHU

For us, initially, this was the number one reason to visit Peru. It is extraordinary! Just make sure you book your ticket at least three months in advance!
Top tip: Aim to climb up Huayna Picchu to get a breathtaking bird's eye view of Machu Picchu (that's a separate ticket that you'll need to also book in advance).

2 → TREK THE INCA TRAIL

This four-day trek in the Andes finishes at Machu Picchu, with a chance afterwards to chill in the natural thermal baths of Aguas Calientes town.
Another top tip: It's so popular that the government limits spaces to just 200 a day, so book at least six months in advance!

3 → VISIT THE ANCIENT CITY OF CUSCO

The beautiful UNESCO-listed historic capital of the Incan Empire is a joy to explore. After the Spanish conquered Peru in the 16th century, they preserved a lot of the Incan buildings whilst adding Baroque churches and palaces to the landscape. Cusco is located pretty high up at 3,500m (11,483ft) altitude.

4 → THE GAY SCENE OF LIMA

There are a handful of gay bars and clubs, mainly concentrated in the districts of tourist-y Miraflores, trendy Barranco, and in downtown Lima. Few survived post-pandemic, but Open Deck and Andel are still standing strong. Lima also has annual LGBTQ+ events like the Marcha del Orgullo Pride Parade in June/July and the Outfest Peru gay film festival also in June.

5 → FOODIE PARADISE IN LIMA

Lima is well-known throughout South America for being a foodie capital. Ceviche (cubed fish marinated in citrus juice) is the most famous Peruvian dish to try. Others include *arroz de chaufa* (fried rice), *tacu tacu* (rice and bean leftovers mixed together), *lomo saltado* (stir fry beef with vegetables) and, our favourite cocktail of all, Pisco Sour!

6 → STAY IN AN AMAZON LODGE

Peru has its own share of the Amazon Rainforest with various jungle lodges to stay in. We headed to Puerto Maldonado, the nearest city to reach the Amazon, where we booked our tour. Alternatively, you can fly to the north of the country to Iquitos and explore the jungle from there.

→ SASHAY WITH PRIDE AROUND THE RAINBOW MOUNTAIN

Yes, a rainbow mountain! The colours are caused by different layers of minerals: red from oxidized iron; brown from oxidized limonite; yellow from iron sulphide; and green/blue from phyllites. The Rainbow Mountain, also known as Vinicunca, can be visited as a day trip from Cusco, but it involves a two-hour trek at 5,000m (16,400ft) altitude, so make sure you've acclimatized first!

01

7 → HIKING COLCA CANYON

One of the deepest canyons in the world, we spent two days hiking around it, staying overnight in an adobe-style bungalow. Along the way we spotted Andean condors, giant hummingbirds, and Chilean flamingos. Arequipa is the nearest city to Colca Canyon (around three hours away), which is also where we arranged our tour.

8 → EXPLORE LAKE TITICACA

Lake Titicaca (try saying that with a straight face!) straddles the border of Peru and Bolivia at an altitude of 3,800m (12,467ft). It is not only the world's highest lake, but also one of the oldest: dating back to over 1 million years! It's also home to many indigenous communities; including the Uros, Taquileños, and Quechua peoples. Puno is the nearest city for boat tours to Lake Titicaca.

9 → ADMIRE THE NAZCA LINES

A series of shapes and figures that the indigenous Nazca people etched into the sands of the Nazca Desert over 2,000 years ago. No one knows why they were built: some say they were part of an irrigation system, others believe they are landing sites for alien spacecraft! The best way to see them is via a short 30-minute flight from the nearby town of Nazca.

Peru has *so much* to offer. From the *dense wonders* of the Amazon Rainforest to the *rich tapestry* of Incan culture in Cusco, from a *tantalizing* array of culinary delights to the budding gay scene in the capital!

OUR PRACTICAL TIPS FOR LGBTQ+ TRAVELLERS

Peru

1 → PERU IS CONSERVATIVE

In relation to LGBTQ+ rights, Peru lags behind its more progressive neighbours – but it's quickly catching up: anti-discrimination laws protecting the LGBTQ+ community were introduced in 2017, and, at the time of print, gay marriage is on the cards.

2 → BE CAUTIOUS WITH PDAS

We advise caution over PDAs unless you're in a gay-friendly environment. Having said that, Peru relies heavily on tourism so gay travellers will feel comfortable and welcome. We had no problems getting a double bed in any of the hotels we stayed at in places like Barranco, Miraflores, Cusco, Arequipa, and Lake Titicaca.

3 → ACCLIMATIZING BASE

Consider using Cusco as a base to acclimatize for a few days before doing any trekking higher up in the mountains. No matter your age or how fit you are, you will inevitably be affected by the altitude – altitude sickness is no joke!

RIGHT One of the floating islands of Lake Titicaca.

COLOMBIA

Colombia has a special place in our hearts. We got engaged here, in Cartagena, in 2017!

**1 → FAVOURITE
GAY CLUB**
Theatron in Bogotá

2 → BEST GAY FESTIVAL
Gay Parade at
Barranquilla Carnival

**3 → FAVOURITE
LANDSCAPE**
Cocora Valley

4 → FAVOURITE TREK
Trails in Tayrona
National Park

**5 → FAVOURITE
MEMORY**
Getting engaged in
Cartagena!

Tourism to Columbia has surged to record levels in recent years, and what was once considered a total no-go area due to internal conflicts between the government, paramilitary groups, and drug cartels, has become a most beloved haven for gay travellers.

Its appeal lies in its diverse offerings: stunning beaches, rich culture, vibrant gay scenes, exciting festivals, breathtaking landscapes, and *some of the hottest people to walk our planet!*

As a gay couple, we never encountered any problems anywhere we went in Colombia. Getting a double bed was never an issue in any of the hotels we stayed in, and they had clearly welcomed LGBTQ+ travellers before. In one hotel we stayed at in Medellín, we noticed a prominent warning sign displaying hefty fines for hate speech against the LGBTQ+ community, reinforcing the country's commitment to inclusivity and acceptance.

And don't forget Theatron in Bogotá: the largest gay club in all of South America. A night out here is an experience you won't forget in a hurry!

Check the latest advice from your local government when planning a trip to Colombia for practical safety tips to consider.

~~~~~~~~~~

LEFT The unique wax palm trees of Cocora Valley in Salento.

OUR TOP EXPERIENCES
Colombia

1 → PARTY IN THEATRON IN BOGOTÁ
It's massive! Every Saturday night up to 5,000 gays head to this mega club. It has thirteen different club rooms spread over five floors, each one catering to a different type of music. Above all else, there is zero attitude at Theatron, which is what we love most about it. Largest gay club in South America? Well, we think it's also certainly *the best* gay club!

2 → GO DANCING AT BARRANQUILLA CARNIVAL
Arguably the gayest event in the country. Whilst not an official gay event, they do dedicate an entire day to the LGBTQ+ community with a colourful Gay Parade. Every gay Colombian guy we met told us this was their favourite queer event. It takes place every February/March.

Gay trivia alert: Barranquilla is also where Shakira is from, *just sayin'. . .*

3 → EXPLORE THE COFFEE TRIANGLE
As coffee aficionados, small towns like Salento and Guatapé in Colombia's central region (also known as the Coffee Triangle) are a delight! Not only is the coffee delicious, but each town is full of character, exuding beauty, charm, and a welcoming ambience.

4 → VISIT EL PEÑÓL DE GUATAPÉ
Close to the colourful town of Guatapé, El Peñol is a huge natural rock standing 200m (650ft) high. Once we conquered the 649 steps (*yup, exactly 649!*) to the top, we were rewarded with a spectacular view across the entire Coffee Triangle region.

5 → SALENTO AND COCORA VALLEY
Close to Salento, the Cocora Valley is famous for its distinctive wax palms that grow up to 200m (656ft) high – making them the tallest palm trees in the world! Salento town was our favourite pueblo (small town) in the Coffee Triangle. Not only is the coffee delicious, but each street is full of charm and character.

6 → GET CULTURAL IN CARTAGENA'S OLD TOWN
It's hard not to fall for the charming UNESCO-listed old town of Cartagena. Every day we went *Insta-crazy* here, exploring the sprawling maze of cobblestone alleys lined with colonial-style mansions, their walls and wooden balconies painted pastel shades of yellow, blue, and green. If you're an artistic queen, go check out the eclectic street art in the Getsemani neighbourhood.

→ FAMOUS GAY COLOMBIAN ICONS
We all know and love Shakira and Maluma. . . but did you know that Conchita Wurst is also Colombian? Created by Austrian Eurovision winner, Thomas Neuwirth, who said that the character of Conchita was born in the mountains of Colombia and got hitched to a French burlesque dancer!

07

7 → MEDELLÍN'S FLOWER FESTIVAL IN AUGUST

Every year, thousands from all around Colombia descend on Medellín for the ten-day Feria de las Flores (Flower Festival). It includes public concerts, pageants, orchid competitions, parades, and tons of parties. It's also very popular with the local gay venues like Viva Auditorium, Purple, and Industry who host various gay flower-themed events during the festival.

8 → TREKKING IN TAYRONA NATIONAL PARK

An ecotourism park located near Santa Marta city up by the Caribbean coast. The park has pristine sandy beaches like Cabo San Juan, which involves a two-hour hike through the tropical rainforest. We loved spotting all the different wildlife on our hike including hummingbirds, toucans, monkeys, and, if you get really lucky, even a snake or two!

Stefan

"AND HE SAID 'YES!'"
◀ *Colombia*

The story of how I asked Seby to marry me!

Seby always boasted to our friends that he would be the one to propose. Each time he took me to a romantic restaurant for a special occasion – our anniversary, my birthday, Valentine's Day – I wondered deep down, *could this be THE moment?*

Yet, with every year that passed us by. . . *nothing!*

So, after eight wonderful years together, I decided to take matters into my own hands.

In May 2017, in Cartagena, I meticulously planned the perfect celebration for Seby's birthday on Sunday 21st.

To start with, I made sure we stayed somewhere special. The boutique adults-only Hotel Quadrifolio fit the bill nicely: housed in a historic Spanish colonial residence in the old town, it felt *correct!*

The plan for the special day was a boat trip exploring the tropical Rosario Islands followed by a romantic evening meal, during which I would ask Seby to marry me.

We stopped at various small islands for some snorkelling. Seby loves being in the water, so I knew this would go down well. Next, we went to Baru Island to chill by the beach. I got us a few Coco Locos – a unique Colombian cocktail where the rum is poured inside the actual coconut to mix with the milk inside. . . *yum!*

For lunch we headed over to Agua Azul Beach Resort. It had excellent reviews for its food, particularly the lobster. It was *good!*

So far, so good: the birthday boy was having a fantastic time, and everything was seamlessly falling into place.

Leaving behind the Rosario Islands, we returned to our hotel to rest, shower, and prepare for what Seby thought was going to be his birthday dinner.

I had chosen the Carmen restaurant because it was renowned for its seven-course taster menu and the location was perfect: set in an elegant colonial house with an intimate outdoor terrace.

The food was really good, but if I'm being honest, I couldn't tell you why nor can I recall what we ate because I was so nervous!

Even though I had rehearsed a thousand times what I wanted to say to Seby in this moment, I was worried. Would this upset him? Would this annoy him? After all, he always said that he wanted to be the one who would propose. I knew in my heart that I was doing the right thing. But I couldn't help feeling anxious throughout the meal.

Instead of rings, I planned to propose with two St. Christopher pendants I had bought before our trip. Neither of us like to wear rings, so I opted for something unique and meaningful to symbolize our engagement. As St. Christopher is the Catholic patron saint of travellers, I

By the end of the meal, most of the other patrons had left and the staff brought a cute birthday cake for dessert, which I had previously requested.

He blew out his candles. . . Here was my chance. . .

"Seby, you know we've been dating now for a long time. And we've been through so much together?"

"Yes, my love," he said with a slightly startled look.

". . .and there is so much more I want to do together. . ."

He broke me off and exclaimed, *"Stefan, are you proposing to me?"*

Seby's face broke out with the biggest smile I've ever seen, his eyes glistened with tears as he looked at me with overwhelming joy.

thought this would be perfect. Although neither of us are remotely religious, I loved what St. Christopher represents – the ideal symbol for the Nomadic Boys!

I was so nervous that I kept putting my hand in my pocket to feel the two pendants to make sure they were still there. My hands were sweating so much from the nerves that I was worried I would ruin the lockets if I touched them too much!

In my mind I was going over the words I had prepared to say to Seby, while at the same time trying to pay attention to him talking: he was excitedly reminiscing about the day's events and I was finding it hard to focus because I was eagerly waiting for the right moment!

"Yes! Yes, I am. . . Seby, I want us to get married. I want to spend the rest of my life with you. What do you say?"

Seby's face broke out with the biggest smile I've ever seen, his eyes glistened with tears as he looked at me with overwhelming joy.

"Oh my god, YES, Stefan, of course I will marry you! I want to spend the rest of my life with you!"

I gave Seby the pendants – one for him and one for me – and explained their meaning. He loved it (*I knew he would*).

He placed his pendant in his wallet for safekeeping, and he carries it with him wherever he goes – a constant reminder of the love and commitment we share.

NORTH AMERICA

Overall, the Americas are a very *gay-friendly pocket* of our planet. Especially Canada, which is often lauded as being "the most gay-friendly country in the world" by various different gay travel pundits. That includes our humble selves! The birth of the modern-day LGBTQ+ movement emanates from the US – from *RuPaul's Drag Race*, Fire Island, Provincetown, Lady Gaga, Folsom, *Sex in the City*, *Will & Grace*. . . we could write a whole book just on this!

Even conservative, Catholic Mexico has very progressive LGBTQ+ laws (including gay marriage) with *über gay havens* in places like Puerto Vallarta and Zona Rosa in Mexico City. To claim that the entire region is gay-friendly, is, of course, naïve of us – the USA is also notorious for harbouring some pretty toxic homophobic forces.

It really does have the two extremes, summed up by the State of Florida: on the one hand you've got Fort Lauderdale and Key West in the south, which are *some of the gayest places we've ever been to.* Yet on the other extreme you've got the abysmal Don't Say Gay campaign and anti-drag laws. . . yup, that's America! But we won't let that stop us from exploring all the great parts North America has to offer.

THE USA (FLORIDA)

The USA, a vast country, offers a lifetime's worth of exploration. Our focus is on Florida, which we've visted multiple times.

1 → BEST GAY SCENE
Wilton Manors, Fort Lauderdale

2 → FAVOURITE GAY RESORT
Island House Resort, Key West

3 → BEST GAY FESTIVAL
St Pete Pride

4 → FAVOURITE GAY BEACH
12th Street Beach in Miami

5 → FAVOURITE RIDE AT UNIVERSAL ORLANDO
The Incredible Hulk Coaster

*H*istorically, Florida is known for being *very gay*, particularly in the southern regions like Key West and Fort Lauderdale. However, recent years have seen the LGBTQ+ community living here in Florida endure a severe backlash under the leadership of Republican Governor Ron DeSantis. During his tenure, the implementation of the abysmal Don't Say Gay laws and attempts to restrict drag performances have marred the state's reputation as a beacon of tolerance.

Whilst it may seem controversial of us to promote Florida in this book when others are advocating to boycott it, we firmly believe that it is now more critical than ever to showcase the resilience and triumphs of the LGBTQ+ community in the Sunshine State. We must stand in solidarity with the local LGBTQ+ community, offering our unwavering support and amplifying their voices against the hate propagated by local authorities under DeSantis.

LEFT A rainbow stroll along Duval Street in Key West.

OUR TOP EXPERIENCES
✈ Florida

1 → THE QUEER SUBURB OF WILTON MANORS
A suburb of Fort Lauderdale and possibly the gayest place on the planet. It's so gay that in 2018 it became the first city in Florida to elect a council entirely comprised of LGBTQ+ members! It's filled to the brim with gay bars, restaurants, clubs, saunas, boutique shops, thrift stores, even gay real estate agents. . . you get the gist! In terms of gay hangouts, we loved the burgers at Rosie's Bar & Grill followed by a drink and boogie at Georgie's Alibi Monkey Bar and Hunters Nightclub.

2 → GET SPOOKED AT THE WICKED MANORS HALLOWEEN PARTY
Our first visit to Fort Lauderdale coincided with this event. No one does Halloween better than Americans, especially gay Americans on the streets of Wilton Manors! The best part is, since the evening outdoor temperature in late October is in the mid-20s, options for outfits are limited only by your imagination!

3 → GAY RESORTS IN FORT LAUDERDALE
Never before had we stayed in a clothing-optional, all-male, all-gay guesthouse until we arrived in Fort Lauderdale. There's quite a few, some of the famous ones include The Worthington Resorts, The Grand Resort and Spa, and the lush Pineapple Point. By day, Fort Lauderdale offers a whole heap of things to do including glorious beaches, day trips to the Everglades and kayaking in Birch Park.

4 → DUVAL STREET IN KEY WEST, FLORIDA
Chilled and Bohemian – is the feeling we got from our first steps on the southernmost part of the US. Duval Street is the gay area of Key West, particularly around the rainbow crossings by 801 Bourbon Bar, Aqua, and the Bourbon Street Pub. If you're here in August, look out for the Tropical Heat five-day festival.

5 → LOSE YOUR MORALS AT THE ISLAND HOUSE RESORT!
An exclusive gay-only resort in Key West, clothing optional, complete with a sauna, steam room, gym, Jacuzzi, hot tub, pool, and, of course, an obligatory darkroom. They are *notorious* for their pool parties on Wednesday and Sunday afternoons, which you can attend on a Day Pass if you're not staying there as an overnight guest.

6 → DRINK BUTTERBEER IN DIAGON ALLEY
Universal Studios in Orlando is *the* best theme park we have ever been to – the rides are *epic*! We spent a whole week here and would happily have stayed longer. The best part was the full recreation of Harry Potter's world with a life-like Diagon Alley and themed rides based on the movies.

7 → PARTY AT ST PETE PRIDE
St Petersburg is the gay hub of West Florida and famous for having the largest gay Pride event in the entire state. It takes place during Pride Month (June) and culminates with a grand parade, live concert, and street party.

8 → GAY BEACHES IN MIAMI
12th Street in Miami Beach is the official gay beach of the city. It's easy to find – located at the intersection of 12th Street and Ocean Drive. Around 16km (10 miles) north of Miami Beach is Haulover Beach, the only clothing-optional beach in Florida. The gay section is between lifeguard towers #15 and #17.

We firmly believe that it is now *more critical* than ever to showcase the *resilience* and *triumphs* of the LGBTQ+ community in the Sunshine State. We must stand in *solidarity* with the local LGBTQ+ community.

OUR USA GAY BUCKET LIST FOR WHEN WE RETURN. . .

✈ *USA*

NEW YORK

Whether it's Hell's Kitchen, Chelsea, West Village, East Village, Lower East Side, Brooklyn, or Harlem, Manhattan feels like it's one of the epicentres of LGBTQ+ culture.

FIRE ISLAND (NEW YORK)

Located two hours from Manhattan just off the coast of Long Island, Fire Island is a gay mecca particularly during the summer months.

PROVINCETOWN (MASSACHUSETTS)

Another gay resort mecca located at the tip of Cape Cod in Barnstable County, Massachusetts. It has one of the largest LGBTQ+ communities in the USA.

PALM SPRINGS (CALIFORNIA)

Gay capital on the West coast where the first White Party was held. What is now a global phenomenon from Bangkok to Miami, the White Party was actually originated in 1989 by gay party organizer Jeffrey Sanker as a humble gathering among friends to fundraise for HIV/AIDS-related charities.

SAN FRANCISCO (CALIFORNIA)

If you grew up reading *Tales of the City* by Armistead Maupin, you'll also have developed a strong desire to visit the Castro gay area of San Francisco.

FOLSOM STREET FAIR (CALIFORNIA)

Every September, this street in San Francisco hosts the *legendary* leather & BDSM event.

ASPEN GAY SKI WEEK (COLORADO)

Widely recognized amongst our fellow skiing friends as being one of *the* best gay ski festivals in the world.

ONE MAGICAL WEEKEND (FLORIDA)

That one time in early June when the world-famous Disney World transforms into four days of gay parties.

WINTER PARTY FESTIVAL IN MIAMI (FLORIDA)

An annual week-long celebration of music and dance on Miami Beach that takes place in late February/ early March.

DALLAS PURPLE PARTY (TEXAS)

The biggest gay circuit party in Texas attracting thousands from all over every May for a weekend of fun.

COACHELLA (CALIFORNIA)

Music and arts festival that takes place in the Colorado Desert every April. Although not a gay-specific event, it regularly features LGBTQ+ artists, and attracts a substantial mixed queer crowd.

→ STONEWALL 50 – WORLDPRIDE NYC 2019: THE LARGEST GAY EVENT IN *HERSTORY*!

New York is home of the modern-day Pride movement, and where the Stonewall Riots happened in 1969. The 50-year celebration of the Stonewall Riots in June 2019 also coincided with New York hosting WorldPride. An estimated 5 million attended, making it the largest gay event in history!

CANADA

Canada's commitment to welcoming gay travellers goes above and beyond. Thankfully, no gay travel advice needed here!

1 → FAVOURITE GAY SCENE
Le Village Gai in Montreal

2 → FAVOURITE GAY SKI FESTIVAL
Whistler Pride & Ski Festival

3 → BEST GAY PRIDE EVENT
Fierté Montréal

4 → FAVOURITE FOOD
Poutine

5 → FAVOURITE MEMORY
Marching in Fierté Montréal with Justin Trudeau!

Where else in the world would you see the (straight, white male) Prime Minister leading a gay pride parade, waving the transgender flag, and crying out "Happy Pride"?

The sight of this heartfelt gesture during Fierté Montréal moved us deeply. The same Justin Trudeau made a spirited guest appearance in the werk room on *Canada's Drag Race: Canada vs. the World* in 2022, showcasing the nation's celebration of diversity and acceptance.

Our personal experiences in Canada revolve around the captivating cities of Toronto, Montreal, Vancouver, and Whistler. Each of these extraordinary places boasts a thriving and vibrant LGBTQ+ community with a large and bustling gay scene, and a calendar brimming with numerous queer events throughout the year.

LEFT Skiing with Pride at the Whistler Pride & Ski Festival.

OUR TOP EXPERIENCES

◢ *Canada*

1 → ATTEND FIERTÉ MONTRÉAL

No one does gay pride quite like Canada. Almost every city has a Pride event often strongly supported (and generously funded) by the local government. Whilst Toronto Pride is the largest gay pride in Canada attracting 1.5 million people, we particularly loved Montreal's. The city has a certain energy that spoke right to our hearts!

2 → LE VILLAGE GAI IN MONTREAL

The largest gay village in North America! Le Village Gai (or simply just The Village) is famous for being the largest gay neighbourhood in North America. It's an entire district of Montreal, which is even officially recognized in tourist city maps. Some of the best hangouts include Sky, Le Stud, Black Eagle, Unity, Stereo, and Cabaret Mado – home of Mado Lamotte, one of the most famous drag queens of Montreal.

3 → TRY POUTINE IN MONTREAL

The perfect hangover cure after a night out in the Gay Village. Poutine is fries with cheese curds topped with gravy. It is *delicious*. The best one we had was at Au Pied de Cochon. Other unique culinary highlights to try in Montreal include smoked meat for dinner at Schwartz's (which is part owned by Celine Dion!) and a Bloody Caesar cocktail (vodka, tomato juice, clamato juice, hot sauce, and Worcestershire sauce).

4 → CHURCH-WELLESLEY VILLAGE IN TORONTO

Just like in Montreal, Toronto has a gay village located at the intersection of Church and Wellesley Streets. Woody's is the largest and most famous gay bar in town. Crews & Tangos is renowned for its drag shows – this was where the Queen of the North herself, Miss Brooke Lynn Hytes, started her career! Other gay hangouts include Black Eagle, The Lodge, The Drink, Pegasus on Church, Garage, and the unique queer theatre Buddies in Bad Times that also hosts parties on weekends.

5 → ADMIRE THE BEAUTY OF NIAGARA FALLS

One of the most famous waterfalls in the world, it is estimated to be around 12,000 years old! Niagara Falls is located 129km (80 miles) from Toronto and shares a land border with New York State, USA. If you rent a car, it takes around one and a half–two hours from Toronto, otherwise it's around three hours by public transport.

→ **CANADA CREATED THE FIRST EVER GAY CURRENCY!**

Well, not quite, but almost – in 2019, Canada unveiled a new $1 coin ($1 coins are nicknamed "loonies" in Canada!) to celebrate the 50th anniversary of the decriminalization of homosexuality. The coin was nicknamed the Equality coin and features two overlapping human faces within a large circle. The words "EQUALITY" and "ÉGALITÉ" also appear on the coin.

07

6 → GO TO WHISTLER PRIDE & SKI FESTIVAL

Canada has many gay ski-based events, including Whistler Pride & Ski Festival in January and Jasper Pride & Ski Festival in April. When we attended Whistler Pride, every day included ski lessons, après ski, shows, and themed parties in the evening. On the final day we took part in a large group rainbow parade where we all skied down the slope together. Whistler is located 121km (75 miles) north of Vancouver, which is the nearest city.

7 → OUTDOOR ADVENTURE IN VANCOUVER AND VANCOUVER ISLAND

If you love the outdoors, you'll love Vancouver. From ocean kayaking to outdoor hikes, the city will feed your lust for adventure. One particular highlight was crossing the 140m (460ft) long suspension bridge at Capilano Park... *phew those views!* Close to Vancouver is Vancouver Island which makes for a fantastic weekend getaway and one of the best places to come for whale watching.

Seby

"DOWN THE BLACK SLOPE WE GO"

⌁ *Canada*

Important life lesson: don't encourage your beginner skier boyfriend to go down the advanced black slopes!

I love skiing.

Growing up in Lyon, I used to ski every weekend during winter with my parents in the French Alps. Nothing beats the feeling of the fresh mountain air as you power down a slope of fresh, powdery white snow. It feels exhilarating – a legal way to get high!

I really wanted Stefan to experience this. So, we decided to go to the Whistler Pride gay ski week.

At the start of the week, we joined the guided groups, which was more for Stefan because I wanted him to learn to ski. I left him in the hands of the instructors and the rest of the beginners whilst I went to the black slopes with the experienced skiers.

Throughout the week, we would reunite in the evenings at the après ski to swap stories. Stefan was excited to demonstrate what he had learned in the morning's class, showcasing his perfected snow plough. His genuine enthusiasm was contagious, especially when he glided down his first blue slope, eagerly awaiting my approval with puppy eyes. Witnessing his sheer joy was exactly what I had hoped for on this trip.

He kept saying his goal was to ski down one of the advanced black slopes together by the end of the week. . .

"We'll see, Stefan. The advanced slopes are pretty challenging and not to be taken lightly by a beginner."

Although I was hesitant, his eagerness and determination won me over.

I pointed up at the least challenging of all the black slopes and said: *"Are you sure you want to do this, Stefan?"*

His eyes sparkled with determination.

"Hell, yeah Seby! Let's DO this. Together!"

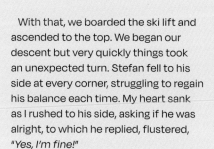

With that, we boarded the ski lift and ascended to the top. We began our descent but very quickly things took an unexpected turn. Stefan fell to his side at every corner, struggling to regain his balance each time. My heart sank as I rushed to his side, asking if he was alright, to which he replied, flustered, *"Yes, I'm fine!"*

Despite his efforts, anxiety overcame him, and his body refused to cooperate.

~~~~~~~~~~

Nothing beats the feeling of the fresh mountain air as you power down a slope of fresh powdery white snow.

~~~~~~~~~~

He tried again but at each corner he would fall to his side. He looked so deflated. I tried to encourage him, but it was as if he'd hit a block and his body refused to move. I felt so bad for him. He only wanted to please me and show off! The remainder of that afternoon was spent cautiously descending on our sides, one slow step at a time.

Finally, after three long hours, we reached the bottom. We were exhausted yet relieved that the ordeal was over. Despite this I was proud of Stefan for giving it his best effort. He simply needed more practice. Before I could suggest returning to the simpler slopes for our next run, he flashed me a cheeky grin and said:

"I think I'll stick to the après ski parties for the remainder of this trip, Seby!"

MEXICO (PUERTO VALLARTA)

**1 → FAVOURITE
GAY EVENT**
Vallarta Pride

**2 → FAVOURITE
GAY BEACH CLUB**
Mantamar Beach
Club Bar

**3 → FAVOURITE
GAY BAR**
Reinas Bar in Zona
Romántica

**4 → FAVOURITE
GAY BRUNCH**
Bistro at Casa Cupula

5 → BEST GAY HOTEL
Almar Resort

*M*exico is a treat, offering a range of wonders like Chichén Itzá, pristine Caribbean coastlines, and a cuisine that is so delectable that UNESCO has rightfully recognized it as an Intangible Cultural Heritage of Humanity.

Mexico also has a lot of *gayness*, particularly in the city of Puerto Vallarta!

For decades, gay travellers (especially from the USA) have been drawn to this charming beach resort town – with some even making it their permanent home! Consequently, the gay scene here has blossomed into an international phenomenon, reaching its peak during the exuberant Vallarta Pride celebrations in May.

We've focused this section on Puerto Vallarta because, to date, it's the only place in Mexico we've visited together. However, we eagerly anticipate returning to explore more of the rich, cultural tapestry of Mexico.

RIGHT Los Muertos Beach in Puerto Vallarta.

Mexico is a *treat*, offering a range of wonders like Chichén Itzá, *pristine* Caribbean coastlines, and a cuisine that is *so delectable* that UNESCO has rightfully recognized it as an Intangible Cultural Heritage of Humanity!

OUR TOP EXPERIENCES

✈ Puerto Vallarta

1 → ZONA ROMÁNTICA

The beating heart and soul of the LGBTQ+ community of Puerto Vallarta. We spent most of our time here, especially in Reinas Bar, La Noche, Divas, and Bar Frida. Gay tour companies like Out Adventures will often include a pub crawl in Zona Romántica as part of their group trips to Puerto Vallarta.

2 → LOS MUERTOS BEACH

The unofficial gay beach of Puerto Vallarta. The main beach bars to check out are Mantamar and Sapphire Ocean Club, which host drag brunches and gay pool parties.

3 → VALLARTA PRIDE

We came to Puerto Vallarta for Pride. It takes place every May to coincide with the US Memorial Day weekend. During Vallarta Pride, all the gay hangouts in Zona Romántica and on Los Muertos beach go all out to create a really fun week with high heel races, drag shows, meet-ups, comedy shows, parties and, of course, the colourful parade through town.

4 → OTHER GAY EVENTS IN PUERTO VALLARTA

Whilst Vallarta Pride dominates, other LGBTQ+ events to look out for include BeefDip Bear Week in January/February, Puerto Vallarta Carnival in February/March, White Party Thanksgiving in November, and even a Gay New Year's Eve party.

5 → GAY HOTELS IN PUERTO VALLARTA

There are many to choose from. Some of the most popular ones include Casa Cupula, Piñata PV Gay Hotel, Hotel Mercurio, Almar Resort, and Jet's Gay Youth Hostel.

RIGHT Some of the fabulous queens at Puerto Vallarta Pride.

→ **SOME HANDY GAY MEXICAN SLANG:**

Activo dominante = a dom top / power top

Pasivo aguantador = a power bottom

Buga = a heterosexual

Chacal = a sexy masculine rough kind of guy who isn't into gay culture

Entrón con lugar = means that the guy you're chatting to can host!

Vergón = a guy who is hung

Morboso = a guy who is very kinky

A pelo = literally means "to hair", but in gay circles means bareback

Bar de ambiente = a cutesy phrase for a gay bar

THE MIDDLE EAST + AFRICA

Whenever we write about the most dangerous places in the world for LGBTQ+ people, they are almost always located in Africa and the Middle East. Most countries in this region have quite terrifying *anti-gay laws* in place, some even imposing the death penalty. That's not to say it's all entirely bad.

South Africa leads the way with one of the most progressive constitutions that *enshrine LGBTQ+ rights* and, as of 2006, was the first (and to date, the only) nation in this region to legalize gay marriage. Israel is another safe haven for LGBTQ+ travellers, although general safety is always something to consider given the instability of the region. Whilst we appreciate safety and moral concerns, we feel it is a shame to completely avoid visiting Africa and the Middle East.

From the pyramids of Giza, safaris in the Maasai Mara, the gay parties of Tel Aviv, trekking Kilimanjaro, the *impressive* site of Petra, the holy atmosphere of Jerusalem's Old City, climbing the world's tallest building – the Burj Khalifa, exploring cosmopolitan Cape Town. . . the list is *endless*. But, as gay travellers, we need to be extra thorough when applying the tips listed in Gay Travel 101 (pages 12–17) when travelling to Africa and the Middle East.

LEBANON

In previous years, Lebanon was considered to be the most gay-friendly country in the Arab World.

*A*t one stage, pre-COVID, Beirut had an abundance of gay bars as well as the largest gay party in the Arab World – despite its anti-gay laws.

However, in a post-COVID world, few LGBTQ+ businesses in Lebanon have survived. Crackdowns on LGBTQ+ organizations have increased over the past few years as the country's ongoing economic and financial crisis has intensified.

Since our visit in 2018, the businesses we mentioned in our online guides on our blog have reached out to us asking us to refer to them as "LGBTQ-friendly" and not "gay" to prevent problems with the local authorities who ruthlessly monitor online activity. We got a flavour of just how vigilant the local authorities are when we were leaving Lebanon on our visit!

LEFT Mohammad Al-Amin Mosque, Beirut.

OUR PRACTICAL TIPS FOR LGBTQ+ TRAVELLERS

We wish we knew all this before our trip!

1 → DON'T RELY ON GETTING YOUR VISA ON ARRIVAL

Apply for your visa from your local Lebanese Embassy before booking your trip – this way, if there is any doubt about your name, the immigration authorities have the chance to "reject" you outright beforehand, thereby minimizing issues when you arrive/leave from Beirut Airport.

2 → GET A SIM CARD AS SOON AS YOU ARRIVE

So that you can make any urgent calls and go online during your trip.

3 → DO NOT POST ANYTHING BEFORE OR DURING YOUR TRIP

The Lebanese government monitors all online activity and will flag anything untoward. Consider putting your accounts on "private".

4 → LEBANON AND ISRAEL ARE OFFICIALLY AT WAR

If you've visited Israel or intend to visit Israel before Lebanon, avoid having an Israeli stamp in your passport – they won't let you in! Get a new passport if you do. Also, scour your social media and remove any posts about Israel.

5 → SAVE THE DETAILS OF YOUR LOCAL EMBASSY IN BEIRUT

Read what your embassy offers in the event of arrest.

6 → TRAVEL INSURANCE IS A MUST FOR ALL TRAVEL TO LEBANON

7 → USE THE VIDEO ON YOUR PHONE AS A WAY TO RECORD CONVERSATIONS

Our local Lebanese friends taught us this: start the video on your phone and then put it in your pocket. This way you have a record of all conversations with the authorities.

8 → ALLOW AT LEAST 3 HOURS FOR BEIRUT AIRPORT

9 → SUPPORT LOCAL LGBTQ+ LEBANESE PEOPLE AND ORGANIZATIONS:

Beirut Pride: Hadi Damien is the founder of Beirut Pride and is doing a terrific job for the LGBTQ+ community of Lebanon. For the 2018 Pride event Hadi was arrested and detained until he was ordered to cancel it. He is active across all social media, particularly on Instagram: *@hadidamien*.

Helem: Another LGBTQ+ rights organization, which was the first of its kind in the Arab world when it was founded in 2001.

LebMASH: An organization of healthcare professionals specializing in the sexual health of marginalized groups including the LGBTQ+ community, women/girls, people living with HIV, and refugees.

"YOUR NAMES ARE BLACKLISTED. YOU SHOULD NOT BE HERE!"

◤ *Lebanon*

We were unfortunately held by Beirut Airport's immigration staff.

We were at Beirut International Airport. We'd spent over an hour waiting to check in for our return flight back to Cyprus followed by another hour in the immigration queue.

Once we *finally* reached the front, Seby was called over, and then me, to the neighbouring booth. I handed over my passport to the immigration officer. He started typing something into his computer and suddenly stopped, gave me a suspicious look, then started saying something in Arabic to his colleague who seemed to have the same issue with Seby. They continued to speak Arabic to each other, each time becoming louder and more frantic. They looked angry.

"Is everything ok?" I asked the man. He looked at me as if he wanted to spit at me and said curtly:

"*You should not be here. You are blacklisted.*"

I was in complete shock. What on earth was going on?!

I looked over at Seby who seemed to be experiencing the same issue. Suddenly I realized this must have something to do with the #*gaylebanon* content we had posted on our social media during our trip for a hotel we were collaborating with in downtown Beirut. There could not be any other possible explanation: my name, Stefan Arestis, with a UK passport is entirely unrelated to Sebastien Chaneac with a French passport. It was more than a mere coincidence.

Had someone at our hotel snitched on us and called up the religious police? It is, after all, a crime to be gay in Lebanon, despite its abundance of queer nightlife. We'd made a rookie "gay travel error" of posting content during our trip!

The two immigration officers now started to argue loudly in Arabic in earshot of all other travellers. It was embarrassing. We felt like criminals.

Another man appeared on the scene wearing a police uniform who must have been their supervisor. He told me and Seby to follow him into his office. Seby grabbed my phone and firmly said to me: "*Stefan remove that rainbow* wallpaper from your phone. Delete all compromising photos/videos especially any of us kissing/cuddling. NOW, quickly!"

We were convinced we would now miss our flight home and be arrested. Were we about to be arrested? Who would we call? What were our rights? Can the British and French Embassies help us? *Our hearts were racing!*

Once inside the immigration policeman's office, the interrogation continued as he looked over our passports:

"Why are you in Lebanon? What are you doing here? What is your job? What is the purpose of your visit? You are blacklisted! You should not be here. You should not have been allowed in the country! What are you doing here?"

We answered each question calmly, explaining we were simply tourists visiting for a short trip to celebrate my birthday. We showed our itinerary – we visited Beirut, did some shopping, visited the sites, and went to the mountains.

However, the man continued with the same questions over and over, almost spitting at us as he spoke. . . *"Your names are blacklisted! You should not be here! What are you really doing here?"*

We repeated the details of our trip, but this seemed to fall on deaf ears.

We tried to ask him what the problem was and if he could explain to us why we were being reprimanded. He ignored us and simply repeated, *"You are blacklisted, you should not be here!"*

Men were coming in and out of the office as the interrogation was happening, each one speaking loudly in Arabic to each other. We kept asking for someone to explain to us what was going on, but nobody would say anything.

It was chaotic. I guess with hindsight they didn't know what to do with us. We'd obviously gotten into the country without any issues, but now that our names were blacklisted, they didn't know if they should retain us, make it an official *thing*, or just let us go.

This lasted for half an hour until the immigration policeman looked us in the eye like we were two naughty children and told us our names are formally blacklisted and we must never return to Lebanon!

Leaving his office, we ran to our gate and managed to board our flight out. We took our seats waiting for the plane to take off. We were so anxious. What if they changed their minds and wanted to keep us longer? They could still board the plane to arrest us. . .

Eventually the plane took off and we were in the air. We could finally breathe!

We never officially found out what the issue was. We started a claim with each of our Embassies, but they were unable to get a response from the Beirut Airport Immigration Police. Interestingly, the hotel we had collaborated with in Beirut had cut all communication with us. They ignored all our emails and telephone calls, which made us suspicious.

Sadly, we found out that other LGBTQ+ bloggers who had since visited Lebanon experienced the same issues with the Immigration Police at Beirut Airport.

Despite our experience leaving Lebanon, we cannot express how much we loved the country, the people and of course, the food! It is truly a joy to explore. However, as with most places in this volatile region of the world, LGBTQ+ travellers have a lot more work to do before they can safely visit.

EGYPT

The allure of the pyramids in Egypt was strong, especially for Seby who's been fascinated about ancient Egypt since he was a child!

1 → MOST MEMORABLE EXPERIENCE
The pyramids!

2 → FAVOURITE FOOD
Feteer

3 → MOST IMPRESSIVE MUSEUM
The Grand Egyptian Museum

4 → BEST MOVIE TO INSPIRE YOUR TRIP
Death on the Nile (2022)

5 → FAVOURITE SOUVENIR
Cartouche oval hieroglyphic necklace

After our traumatic experience leaving Lebanon in 2018, we decided to avoid all travel to countries with anti-gay lawzs, particularly as our online profile depicting us as two very out-and-proud gay guys continued to grow.

However, unlike Lebanon, Egypt seems to have embraced gay travellers a little better. For example, there are many tour operators offering gay trips here; we couldn't find any similar opportunities in Lebanon.

In addition, the largest gay cruise company in the world, Atlantis, includes Egypt as one of its stop overs in its Mediterranean voyage. Knowing this helped alleviate our fears: if something as *gay* as Atlantis Cruises docks in Egypt, then surely, we'd be ok too, *right*?

Unlike our trip to Lebanon, we decided to book a private guide for the entirety of our trip. We're so glad that we did. Our guide met us as soon as we got off the plane, guided us through customs and security, and then accompanied us throughout our trip.

In addition, we were armed with a lot more practical knowledge off the back of our experience in Lebanon – we were careful to post nothing about our trip before and during our time in Egypt. We avoided all PDAs and blocked people from Egypt from being able to access our website. We also scoured our social media, deleting all posts relating to Egypt. As a result, we were absolutely fine and ended up having an incredible time!

OUR TOP EXPERIENCES

1 → GO POTTY FOR PYRAMIDS!
Despite being over 4,000 years old, they still stand proud today and they dominate Giza's skyline. They were built in around 2500 BC by the pharaohs of the ancient Egyptian Empire. The Sphinx statue is another not-to-miss structure, situated close to the pyramids.

2 → THE MUMMIES HALL IN THE NATIONAL MUSEUM OF EGYPTIAN CIVILIZATION
This is just as impressive as the pyramids. The mummified bodies of the pharaohs have been preserved and housed in this museum in Cairo. It's mind blowing – almost chilling – to see the body of a person so close up from over 4,000 years ago!

3 → GRAND EGYPTIAN MUSEUM IN GIZA
The largest museum in the world, and still in construction when we visited in September 2023. It houses all of the treasures found in the tomb of King Tutankhamun such as his famous golden masks, chariots, sarcophagi, and around 7,000 other pieces of treasure.

4 → VALLEY OF THE KINGS IN LUXOR
The Valley of the Kings was a royal burial ground for nobles and pharaohs during the New Kingdom (1570–1085 BC) including Tutankhamun, Seti I, and Ramses II. The entire area is still an active archaeological site where Egyptologists continue to make discoveries.

5 → CRUISE ON THE NILE
This is a rewarding way to experience Egypt. Most cruises start in Luxor and head down to Aswan. They can be done over 3–7 nights depending on the itinerary and number of stops you do along the way.

6 → ABU SIMBEL TEMPLE
Comprising two massive rock-cut temples in the village of Abu Simbel in southern Egypt, close to the Sudan border. It was constructed as a place for people to worship Pharaoh Ramses II as a god following his death. The outside of the temple features four colossal 20m (66ft) seated statues of Ramses II.

7 → DIVING IN THE RED SEA
For many divers, the Red Sea is up there as one of the most impressive diving sites, teeming with beautiful coral reefs and rich marine life. The water is clear and pristine because no rivers enter it. The most popular places to base yourself for diving are Hurghada or Sharm El-Sheikh.

→ THE FIRST EVER RECORDED GAY COUPLE IN HISTORY IS FROM ANCIENT EGYPT!
Khnumhotep and Niankhkhnum were both highly esteemed royal servants of Pharaoh Niuserre (around 2380–2320 BC) during the 5th Dynasty. They were buried together in the same tomb in Saqqara. Their tomb also contained several paintings of the two men embracing each other and touching their faces nose-on-nose, which was a form of kissing in ancient Egypt.

OUR PRACTICAL TIPS FOR LGBTQ+ TRAVELLERS

✈ *Egypt*

1 → HIRE A REPUTABLE GUIDE

Either visit Egypt on one of the gay tours or, if you can't make their specific dates, reach out to these companies (such as Out Adventures, HE Travel, Brand g, and Detours) and ask for their recommendation for a gay-friendly guide. Sadly, our guide requested to be kept anonymous for his safety asking us only to recommend him privately.

2 → THE EGYPTIAN POLICE USE GRINDR

When you open the app in Egypt, Grindr sends you a pop-up message warning you to be careful because local police actively use the app to target gay men and arrest them! Always ask for their social media channels before meeting anyone on Grindr and insist on a quick video call so that you can verify their identity.

3 → THERE IS NO GAY SCENE

Local gay Egyptian guys told us that our best bet for a queer-friendly space would be international hotel bars like the Marriott.

4 → BUY SOME ANTINAL

As soon as you arrive, go to any pharmacy and buy these inexpensive local pills. *Trust us*! Unlike Imodium, Antinal also targets local bacteria that enter your gut. As soon as an upset stomach hits, you'll be glad you had Antinal to hand. Both of us were hit with the runs on our second day, and thanks to Antinal we were quickly able to recover without it hindering our tour.

～～～～～～～～～～～

RIGHT The Sphinx, the pyramids, and the Nomadic Boys!

ISRAEL

"Tel Aviv is the gayest place on the planet!" said every straight Israeli we'd ever met, and we were thrilled to experience it.

1 → BEST GAY EVENT
Tel Aviv Pride

2 → FAVOURITE GAY BEACH
Hilton Beach

3 → FAVOURITE GAY CLUB
Haoman 17

4 → FAVOURITE MEMORY
Exploring the Old City of Jerusalem

5 → MOST UNIQUE EXPERIENCE
Floating in the Dead Sea

When it comes to LGBTQ+ rights, Israel is a trailblazer compared to all its neighbouring Middle Eastern countries. It is the only safe place for gay people in the region, a place where we felt completely safe as a gay couple, especially in Tel Aviv. PDAs were never a problem and none of the hotels had an issue hosting a gay couple.

Beyond the gay scene of Tel Aviv, Israel has an array of captivating sites to explore. The Old City of Jerusalem left an indelible mark on our hearts, standing out as one of the highlights of our journey. Moreover, the country boasts a plethora of natural wonders and activities, including the unique experience of relaxing in the buoyant waters of the Dead Sea.

Take note that in Israel, their weekend (Shabbat) spans from Thursday evening to Saturday night, and most individuals resume work on Sunday.

→ TRAVEL ADVICE NOTE
Please check the latest advice from your local government before travelling to Israel to make sure it is safe to visit.

OUR TOP EXPERIENCES

1 → TEL AVIV PRIDE

The mother of all gay events, thanks to the epic parties like PAPA Party, Forever Tel Aviv, and Matinée's Pervert Party. The Pride event also hosts live concerts – the most popular is the Offer Nissim concerts, who performs at every Tel Aviv Pride and guarantees a sell out! The parade itself attracts around 250,000 people a year.

2 → GAY BEACHES IN TEL AVIV

Every single one of those ripped Israeli guys you've chatted with on Grindr on your way into the city from Ben Gurion Airport will likely be on Hilton Beach (in front of the Hilton Tel Aviv Hotel) clad in tight speedos. This is the cruisiest spot in the whole city! For a more clothing-optional gay beach experience, head up to Ga'ash gay beach, which is located 19km (12 miles) north of Tel Aviv (around 40 minutes by local bus, and quicker by taxi).

3 → GAY BARS OF TEL AVIV

When researching Tel Aviv for our visit, the gay scene seemed tiny at first: there is no official gay area and just two gay bars – Shpagat and Layla. But that's because the entire city is so gay that almost any bar will have a large concentration of gay people.

4 → GAY CLUBS IN TEL AVIV

The highlights of the gay scene are the weekly parties that take place at clubs like Lima Lima Bar and Haoman 17 (a chain of clubs). The most popular parties at Haoman include Ofra Bli Ofra and PAG. Look out for the larger themed circuit parties hosted by Forever Tel Aviv throughout the year, especially during Pride.

5 → OLD CITY OF JERUSALEM

Nothing beats the feeling of getting lost in the labyrinth of narrow cobblestone streets in a place that dates back to at least 3000 BC. It is remarkable – you *feel* an energy in the air here! This is one of the holiest places in the world and a pilgrimage for Jews, Christians, and Muslims. UNESCO lists 220 historic monuments to visit including Temple Mount, the Dome of the Rock, and the Western Wall. We recommend a day trip to Bethlehem, which is 9½km (6 miles) away (around 15 minutes by car and 1 hour by local bus).

6 → FLOATING IN THE DEAD SEA

The first thing we noticed was the unmistakable tang of salt. *Avoid getting it in your eyes*! The Dead Sea is around 10 times saltier than normal seawater, which makes it almost impossible to swim in. However, it is ideal to simply lie back and float on, which makes for a relaxing and energizing experience thanks to the rich minerals in the water.

SOUTH AFRICA

South Africa shines as a beacon of LGBTQ+ rights and acceptance on the entire African continent.

1 → BEST GAY EVENT
Johannesburg Pride

2 → FAVOURITE GAY BEACH
Clifton 3rd, Cape Town

3 → FAVOURITE TREK
Platteklip Gorge,
Table Mountain

4 → FAVOURITE MEMORY
Safari at Pilanesberg
National Park

5 → BEST SOUVENIR
Handmade traditional
African jackets from
Caraci Clothing

*I*n a groundbreaking move led by Nelson Mandela in 1995, South Africa became the world's first country to enshrine LGBTQ+ rights in its constitution. Continuing this legacy of progress, it proudly stands as the first and only nation in Africa to legalize gay marriage in 2006.

Cape Town is our favourite place in South Africa. Nestled along the coast, embraced by the majestic Table Mountain, it offers a breathtaking setting. There is also an active gay scene in the De Waterkant district.

Cape Town exudes charm; Johannesburg, on the other hand, presents a more rugged and edgy vibe. The city boasts its own array of gay hangouts scattered throughout, and it proudly hosts Africa's largest gay event, Johannesburg Pride, in October. Notably, Johannesburg also serves as a convenient base for embarking on thrilling safari tours in the surrounding national parks.

→ SOUTH AFRICAN PRIDE MONTH

October is Pride Month in South Africa due to the historic South African pride parade held on 13th October 1990 in Johannesburg. This milestone event marked the first-ever pride march on the entire African continent, solidifying South Africa's pioneering role in advancing LGBTQ+ rights and celebrations.

RIGHT Embracing our Pride with Sebo in the Maboneng neighbourhood of Johannesburg.

OUR TOP EXPERIENCES

↗ *South Africa*

1 → HANDMADE TRADITIONAL AFRICAN JACKET FROM CARACI

The best part of our trip! Sebo is a gay local in Johannesburg who set up Caraci Clothing and makes handmade traditional African jackets from fabric that he picks out for you. Not only is this an incredible souvenir, but Sebo was a joy to be around who told us all about gay life in Johannesburg and what it was like growing up in a township.

2 → VISIT A TOWNSHIP

A sad reminder of the Apartheid era. Black and brown people were separated into mini-cities called "townships" and kept away from city centres. Townships were often neglected by the authorities and were therefore ridden with violence and poverty. Soweto is one of the most famous because it's where Nelson Mandela lived in 1946–1962 and can be visited as part of a guided tour.

3 → SPOTTING THE BIG FIVE IN A SAFARI

Lions, leopards, elephants, rhinos, and buffalos make up the Big Five. We based ourselves at a lodge near the Pilanesberg National Park for 3 days/2 nights and over this period we managed to see all five during our safaris, along with many other animals. Pilanesberg National Park is 217km (135 miles) from downtown Johannesburg and it took us just under 3 hours to drive there.

4 → HIKING ON TABLE MOUNTAIN

No visit to Cape Town is complete without a trek on Table Mountain. There are several trails to do, each of varying difficulty and length. Our advice is to set out early in the day and avoid returning in the dark. There is a cable car for the return leg if you want to rest. The highlight is the views of the city below and the dramatic Atlantic coastline surrounding it.

5 → THE GAY SCENE OF CAPE TOWN

The chic district of De Waterkant in Cape Town is where the bulk of the city's LGBTQ+ community is based with bars like Café Manhattan, Zer021 Rooftop, and clubs like The Pink Candy, Evol, and Stargayzers.

6 → GAY EVENTS IN SOUTH AFRICA

Johannesburg Pride in October is the largest LGBTQ+ event in not only South Africa, but in the whole of Africa. It's so iconic that it's been nicknamed "The Pride of Africa". Over in Cape Town, the Pride event coincides with Carnival season in February/March. Another big event to take place that is popular with the LGBTQ+ community of South Africa is Rocking the Daisies. It's a music festival that takes place every October in both Cape Town and Johannesburg.

LEFT Hiking in Cape of Good Hope near Cape Town.

OCEANIA

Oceania will reward you with *unique landscapes*, wildlife, adventure, and some of the gayest places on Earth (*wink, wink, Sydney!*). Seby's dream was to one day be able to see the underwater life of the Great Barrier Reef; Stefan's, to meet a kangaroo. In September 2023, we finally got the chance to realize our Down Under dreams. And *oh boy* were we spoilt!

We had a blast partying in gay Sydney. We were in awe swimming with manta rays, sharks, and turtles in the Great Barrier Reef. Our *jaws dropped* at the impressive vistas during our "tramping" (the Kiwi word for hiking) experiences in New Zealand. We were spellbound by the *peace and serenity* of the Fjordlands. We got to live out our *Lord of the Rings* fantasies whilst exploring the Shire at the Hobbiton movie studios.

Our only regret is that Oceania cannot be explored in one short trip. You'd need to spend months – if not years – to *fully discover* it. You'd better believe we're already planning our next visit!

↗ Oceania

AUSTRALIA

For years, we've wanted to visit the Kingdom of Kylie! As soon as Australia joined Eurovision in 2015, we took it as a sign.

1 → BEST GAY EVENT
Sydney Mardi Gras

2 → FAVOURITE GAY BEACH
Cobblers Beach

3 → OUR CULTURAL HIGHLIGHT
A show at the
Sydney Opera House

4 → TOP GAY PARTY
The Beresford on
Sundays in Sydney

5 → OUR FAVOURITE MEMORY
Swimming with
manta rays in the
Great Barrier Reef

I grew up dreaming about one day diving in the rich waters of the Great Barrier Reef. For Stefan, he's been obsessed with Australia since he was a young, gay kid: he knew all the words to Kylie's *and* Danni's songs. The iconic *The Adventures of Priscilla, Queen of the Desert* was one of his favourite movies, and every day after school he'd tune into *Neighbours* and *Home and Away*.

So, when the spotlight of the gay world was on Sydney for WorldPride in early 2023, we knew it was also our time to finally visit.

The problem with Australia is that you simply can't appreciate it in its entirety on a small 2- or 3-week trip. This country is massive, almost the same size as Europe. Ideally, you'd want to dedicate *at least* one month and travel by car through the country. However, for gay travellers on their first visit, we've hit up some of the top things we think you should aim to cover!

LEFT Sunrise over the Sydney
Opera House.

OUR TOP EXPERIENCES

✈ *Australia*

1 → THE GAY SCENE OF SYDNEY

Sydney is EXPLODING with gays! Particularly the gay triangle bubble between the suburbs of Darlinghurst, Potts Point, and Surry Hills. Note that bars in Sydney are referred to as "Hotels" and most double up as clubs! Stonewall Hotel and Oxford Hotel are the main ones, but our favourite is The Beresford. Sydney also has several gay beaches that are a short Uber ride away such as Obelisk, Cobblers, and La Perouse.

2 → PARTY HARD AT SYDNEY MARDI GRAS

The Mother of all gay festivals in all of Oceania and one of Australia's biggest annual festivals! Sydney's Mardi Gras takes place during carnival season in February/March.

3 → GO TO SYDNEY HARBOUR

Home to one of the most recognizable landmarks in the world: the Sydney Opera House and Harbour Bridge. Our favourite moment was watching the sunrise here during a morning run. For the best view of the harbour at sunset, we recommend heading to Mrs Macquarie's Chair next to the Botanic Garden.

4 → THE GAY SCENE OF MELBOURNE

Often lauded as Australia's cultural hub, with a vibrant LGBTQ+ community to match Sydney's, some of the best bars and parties include The Laird, Prince Public Bar, Poof Doof, and Sircuit. The city's largest LGBTQ+ event is the Midsumma Festival (Jan/Feb).

5 → SCUBA DIVING IN THE GREAT BARRIER REEF

As keen divers, this was top of our Aussie Bucket List. It's hands down the best diving we've ever done! We went to Lady Elliot Island which is famous for its resident manta rays. We managed to stay at its sole eco-resort, which gets booked up months ahead! Interestingly, we also spotted a large number of LGBTQ+ families here.

6 → TAKE A PRISCILLA-INSPIRED ROAD TRIP

The 1994 movie *The Adventures of Priscilla, Queen of the Desert* is one of the most famous gay movies ever made. It follows two drag queens and a transgender woman driving from Sydney to Alice Springs in the middle of Australia.

7 → ADMIRE ULURU (AYERS ROCK)

Uluru is the world's largest monolith located right in the heart of Australia. It is a UNESCO-listed, large, natural sandstone formation and is sacred to the Pitjantjatjara people. The surrounding area is also home to wildlife such as thorny devils, dingoes, kangaroos, wallabies, and emus. Visiting involves flying to Alice Springs airport, followed by a five-hour drive.

8 → VISIT THE QUIRKY MONA OF TASMANIA

The Museum of Old and New Art (MONA) is famous for being one of the quirkiest museums in the world due to its focus on sex and death, giving it the nickname of a "subversive adult Disneyland"!

9 → THE MOST AGGRESSIVE CROCODILES IN THE WORLD!

The Australian saltwater crocodiles are fierce! You can go on a "jumping croc cruise" near Darwin in the Northern Territory. The tour is so named because the guide will tie some raw meat to a stick and hang it over the water. The crocs then literally jump up out of the water to snap the food!

OUR PRACTICAL TIPS
FOR LGBTQ+ TRAVELLERS

1 → CUSTOMS IS STRICT
Declare any medication you're bringing. Don't bring any food from the plane. Also, be prepared to declare things like PrEP medication on your landing card. We found the queue for declaring items at Sydney Airport was a lot shorter and quicker than the "No Items To Declare" queue.

2 → JAYWALKING IS ILLEGAL
And you can get a fine if caught. Just wait for the green man before crossing to be on the safe side.

3 → BE AWARE OF TIME ZONE ALTERATIONS
Almost every region of Australia has its own time zone. Each time you move to a new city we recommend manually setting the local time on your phone (because if you've turned roaming off, this automatic setting won't work without the internet).

→ EVER TRIED A GAY ICE CREAM?
Golden Gaytime is one of the most famous ice creams in Australia and it's good! Why? Because it tastes of unicorns and rainbows! Only teasing. . . but you can't say you've been to Australia until you've tried a Golden Gaytime. . . we are living for their crumbly exterior and smooth interior!

Oceania

NEW ZEALAND

"Seby, one day we're going to go to New Zealand and run through the Shire just like Frodo and Sam!"

1 TOP LGBTQ+ EVENT
Winter Pride in
Queenstown

**2 → OUR
FAVOURITE HIKE**
Ben Lomond Track,
Queenstown

**3 → TOP ROMANTIC
EXPERIENCE**
Overnight cruise in
Doubtful Sound

**4 → OUR
FAVOURITE TOUR**
The Hobbiton movie set

**5 → MOST UNIQUE
ACTIVITY**
Stargazing in Mount
Cook's Dark Sky Reserve

For us, *The Lord of the Rings* movies were our first taste of New Zealand. The rolling green hills and breathtaking landscapes provided director Peter Jackson with the ideal backdrop to recreate Tolkien's Middle-earth. Those rugged landscapes that inspired so many movies are also prime for "tramping" (the New Zealand word for hiking). And if it's wild adrenaline adventures you seek, you're in the right place!

New Zealand is also very gay-friendly. We found Kiwis to be relaxed and accepting. Not once did we experience any issues. For years, they've been trailblazers of LGBTQ+ rights: as far back as 1993, they introduced anti-discrimination laws along with the legal right to change your gender, and in 2013 they became the first nation in the Asia-Pacific region to legalize gay marriage. They've had openly LGBTQ+ politicians for years, the most prominent being Georgina Beyer who, in 1995, became the world's first openly transgender mayor (of Carterton), as well as the world's first openly transgender Member of Parliament.

When it comes to gay parties, New Zealand is not as internationally renowned as its big Aussie sister. Instead, be prepared to be *blown away* by Mother Nature, *whilst living out your Middle-earth fantasy!*

OUR PRACTICAL TIPS FOR LGBTQ+ TRAVELLERS

1 → CUSTOMS IS STRICT!
New Zealanders love their environment and wildlife and fight hard to protect them. Taking any food and drink into the country is banned – custom officers will want to inspect things like your walking shoes and medication. Our advice for your landing card – if in doubt about anything you have, just declare it to be on the safe side.

2 → DON'T BRING A DRONE
They are banned almost everywhere throughout the country.

3 → DON'T UNDERESTIMATE THE WEATHER
The New Zealand weather changes dramatically every day and can be quite unpredictable. As a result, some activities will be cancelled so make sure you're flexible with last minute cancellations and have adequate travel insurance.

4 → TRANSLATE YOUR DRIVING LICENCE
If there is anything non-English on your driving licence, car rental companies may refuse to rent you a car unless you have a translation. We were recommended this efficient translation service who can digitally translate your licence within 24 hours for a fee of around £30: www.TransNational-ltd.co.nz.

→ GAY ACCOMMODATION IN NEW ZEALAND
If you're searching for LGBTQ+ owned or managed accommodation in New Zealand, we recommend checking out www.gaystay.co.nz. It's the most comprehensive directory we've found listing all LGBTQ+ options across the country, including clothing-optional, men-only, lesbian and trans hosts.

RIGHT Exploring the Shire at the Hobbiton movie set.

OUR TOP EXPERIENCES

✈ *New Zealand*

1 → ATTEND WINTER PRIDE AND SKI FESTIVAL

This is the biggest, annual queer event on South Island, taking place over ten days in August/September in Queenstown. As well as skiing, it also includes themed party nights, shows, dinners, and a Pride Ski Flag Parade.

2 → GET YOUR SHOT OF ADRENALINE IN QUEENSTOWN

Nicknamed the "adventure capital of the world", Queenstown is a paradise for thrill seekers. There are many different bungee jumps and swings to try. The Nevis Swing is famous for being the world's biggest swing, but we prefer the Shotover Canyon where you can choose your jump style – on a chair, upside down, or even backwards!

3 → TRAMPING AROUND NEW ZEALAND

For us, nothing beats the 360-degree mountain top views during our trek to Ben Lomond Summit in Queenstown, or the Hooker Valley Track hike by Mount Cook.

4 → OVERNIGHT CRUISE IN THE FJORDLANDS

This region of South Island is breathtaking – particularly Milford Sound. However, the only way to see it is on one of the many cruises, which are usually busy. For a more peaceful and serene experience, we recommend an overnight cruise to Doubtful Sound.

5 → DISCOVER MĀORI CULTURE IN ROTORUA

We recommend the three-hour experience at Te Puia which includes a cultural show and a *hāngi* (a traditional Māori banquet). Rotorua is also famous for its geothermal activity.

The hot springs, mud pools, and geysers are considered sacred sites by the Māori. We recommend booking a Geothermal Walk and Mud Bath Experience at Hell's Gate.

6 → THE GAY SCENE OF AUCKLAND

With the largest LGBTQ+ community in New Zealand, this is the best place to let your hair down. The gay hangouts are concentrated along the gritty Karangahape Road (nicknamed "K-Road") and include Eagle Bar, G.A.Y Auckland, Caluzzi Cabaret, Family Bar, and Centurian Sauna. The Auckland Pride Festival in February is the city's largest annual LGBTQ+ event. The Big Gay Out open-air event also takes place in February.

7 → EXPLORE THE SHIRE IN HOBBITON

The Hobbiton Movie Set is where you can see Bag End up close. With tours leaving every 20 minutes, it gets super busy, so we recommend booking the first or last tour of the day to avoid the crowds.

8 → SEE KIWIS IN THE WILD ON STEWART ISLAND

Nature is in charge here, and it is dominated by birds, in particular the small kiwi birds (found nowhere else!) that New Zealanders are nicknamed after.

9 → STARGAZING IN MOUNT COOK

The darkness of the night sky and minimal light pollution around Mount Cook makes it one of the best places in the country for stargazing. We recommend a stargazing tour (all hotels in the area offer it) and to download one of the stargazing apps (like Stellarium or Star Chart).

03

10 → THE GLOW WORM CAVES OF WAITOMO

Glow worms are in fact the larvae of the fungus gnat and not actual worms! They hang from the roof of dark, damp caves, suspended in their cocoons, and produce a soft light to attract smaller insects for food. Nothing beats gliding on a raft through the the Waitomo Glowworm Caves in the dark, underneath the Milky Way-like greenish glow!

11 → WATER SPORTS IN THE BAY OF ISLANDS

In the summer months people head here for kayaking, sailing, paddleboarding, fishing, and even diving. Another highlight is a whale watching tour where you can spot dolphins, orcas, and whales in the wild.

OUR GLOBAL FAMILY

As we conclude our journey through these pages, we sincerely hope that our stories have ignited a spark of inspiration.

*B*efore we part ways, there is one final sentiment we want to share: the pride and love we feel for our worldwide LGBTQ+ community. Perhaps this may sound obvious, but in every new place we visit we always find an LGBTQ+ community living there, resilient and determined, transcending local laws and social norms that seek to suppress them.

It's often easy to forget that gay people exist in places like Russia, Uganda, Yemen, and Saudi Arabia, where governments have enacted terrifying anti-gay laws, forcing them into the shadows, back in the closet.

> *Positive change begins when we openly engage in these discussions, fostering empathy and understanding.*

Some may argue, *"How dare you spend money in a country that wants to throw us in jail?"*, a sentiment we often encounter online. Yet, by resorting to complete boycotts, we inadvertently deny ourselves the opportunity to help the local LGBTQ+ community, who deserve our support the most. We spend our money in businesses owned and operated by LGBTQ+ individuals and those that are genuinely gay-friendly.

Through our travels, we have come to realize that true power lies in supporting the local LGBTQ+ community and, whenever it is safe to do so, giving them the visibility they deserve.

By empowering them to say, *"Hi, I'm here!"* in the face of oppressive governments trying to suppress them, we spark essential conversations. Positive change begins when we openly engage in these discussions, fostering empathy and understanding.

We take pride in being a vital part of this discussion, standing alongside our LGBTQ+ family around the world.

INDEX

ACKNOWLEDGEMENTS

We want to express our deepest gratitude to everyone who has taken the time to read, share, comment on our content and follow us on our journey since we began Nomadic Boys in 2013. This book is for you!

We couldn't have undertaken this journey without the backing and drive of the publishing team at Pavilion. We also thank our literary agent, David H. Headley, whose advice was invaluable.

And, of course, to each other. Nomadic Boys is one of the greatest achievements to come out of our relationship and we're dead proud of it.

→ **STEFAN**

When writing, you always have a single ideal first reader in mind who you feel like you're telling the story to. For me that is my awesome sister Natalie. She's always had my back and supported me through everything. I love and respect her dearly. Special shout out to my cheeky nephews, Alec and Callum – always on hand to offer useful quips at every stage of the writing. And, of course, to my wonderful parents, Maro (RIP) and Philip.

→ **SEBY**

From a young age I have been plotting my every move with my best friends Marie, Marion, and Johan to hand. They've inspired and supported me through life as have my awesome family, in particular my mother, Christiane, my father, Jean Luc, my twin sister Magali and older brothers Stephane and Lionel.

→ **ONE LOVE, ENDLESS ADVENTURES**

We love interacting with our readers, so reach out on our website and social media – and let's travel the world together!

www.nomadicboys.com
@nomadicboys

First Published in the United Kingdom in
2024 by Pavilion
An imprint of HarperCollins*Publishers* Ltd
1 London Bridge Street
London SE1 9GF

www.harpercollins.co.uk

HarperCollins*Publishers*
Macken House
39/40 Mayor Street Upper
Dublin 1
D01 C9W8
Ireland

10 9 8 7 6 5 4 3 2 1

First published in Great Britain by Pavilion
An imprint of HarperCollins*Publishers* 2024

Copyright © Pavilion 2024
Text © Stefan Arestis and Sebastien
Chaneac 2024

Stefan Arestis and Sebastien Chaneac assert
the moral right to be identified as the authors
of this work. A catalogue record of this book
is available from the British Library.

ISBN 978-0-00-860415-8

This book contains FSC™ certified paper
and other controlled sources to ensure
responsible forest management.

For more information visit:
www.harpercollins.co.uk/green

Publishing Director: Stephanie Milner
Commissioning Editor: Kiron Gill
Project Editor: Francesco Piscitelli
Editorial Assistant: Shamar Gunning

Design Manager: Laura Russell
Junior Designer: Lily Wilson
Layout Designer: Kei Ishimaru
Production Controller: Grace O'Byrne
Proofreader: John Friend
Indexer: Vanessa Bird
D&I Reader: Davina Bhanabhai

Printed and bound by Rotolito S.P. A. in Italy

Photo credits
Shutterstock: pages 26, 29, 47, 61, 71, 82,
86 & 135.

Stefan Arestis and Sebastien Chaneac: pages
2, 4, 5, 6, 9, 10, 13, 15, 16, 20, 31, 36, 39, 43, 50,
56, 63, 66, 69, 72, 78, 80, 84, 92, 96, 100, 103,
105, 106, 108, 115, 122, 130, 133, 136, 139, 144,
146, 150, 153, 157, 159, 162, 169, 173, 174, 178,
181, 183, 185, 186 & 191.

We are committed to respecting the
intellectual right of others. We have therefore
taken all reasonable efforts to ensure that the
reproduction of all contents on these pages
is done with the full consent of the copyright
owners. If you are aware of unintentional
omissions, please contact the company
directly so that any necessary corrections
may be made for future editions.